SAKHEE BOOK

SAKHEE BOOK

OR

THE DESCRIPTION OF

GOOROO GOBIND SINGH'S RELIGION AND DOCTRINES,

TRANSLATED FROM GOOROO MUKHI INTO HINDI,

AND AFTERWARDS INTO ENGLISH.

SIRDAR ATTAR SINGH.

CHIEF OF BHADOUR

GYAN

Published by

GYAN

Gyan Publishing House
5, Ansari Road
Daryaganj, New Delhi-110002
Phone: 011-47034999, 9811692060
E-mail: books@gyanbooks.com

Distribution Network
gyanbooks.com
India, USA, Canada, UK, Australia, France

ISBN : 978-81-212-9432-4 (PB)
First Published, 1873

2nd Impression 2023

Printed at: Gyan Press, Delhi.

SAKHEE BOOK
Translator: SIRDAR ATTAR SINGH

SAKHEE BOOK

OR

THE DESCRIPTION OF

GOOROO GOBIND SINGH'S

RELIGION AND DOCTRINES,

TRANSLATED FROM GOOROO MUKHI INTO HINDI,

AND AFTERWARDS INTO ENGLISH.

BY

SIRDAR ATTAR SINGH,

CHIEF OF BHADOUR

BENARES:

PRINTED AT THE MEDICAL HALL PRESS.

1873.

TRANSLATOR'S PREFACE.

Oh! how wonderful is the creation of God that above all wordly things, religion is the supreme thing. With its corruption, the corruption and degeneration of all things generally happen; for, it is religion that binds thousands in one cord of union. It is the saying of the sage, that religion and secular things are the twins. It is owing to disunion in religion, that rebellion and other disturbance in the country generally happen. The learned foreigners have justly separated religion from legislation. But the real and true management of a country depends upon the strength of religion. Such points of nicities are generally observed by those who are learned and experienced and who are in short, able statesmen to govern a country. Such benign government as this, is an act of kindness of the Almighty, and the management of such a country entirely depends upon human beings.

DESCRIPTION OF THE TRANSLATION.

This work was originally written in Hindi prose and poetry. The meanings generally differed from the rules of Grammar and as a matter of course, men of shallow intellect and understanding generally misunderstood those ambiguous meanings and phrases. But such misunderstood words and phrases were considered as words of prophecy, and hence they (the ignorant) always failed to comprehend what the original meanings are. I have tried my best to translate into English those words and phrases with clearness and accuracy. There are words in this book so arranged and placed under the rules of Rhetoric and Syntax that when they are closely read and consulted, they imply that some rebellion will soon happen. It is for this reason that the book is considered strange and uncommon even by the learned sometimes. All these will be evident to the reader when they will peruse it.

DESCRIPTION OF WORDS OF THIS BOOK.

In this book there are generally three kinds of words, viz. 1*st*, the author's use of significant words of Sakhee; 2*nd*, the author's use of such words which others could not comprehend, and hence the difference of opinions among them; 3*rd*, the author's use of ambiguous words which excite doubt and curiosity. But as far as I can, I have used words that convey true and precise meaning. He will be the true judge of this book who will read the original Hindi work written in prose and poetry. This translation will not explain the ambiguity which is in the original. In order to explain such ambiguity I have given foot notes.

BOOK OF FAITH.

This book contains the true discription of the Seikh religion, and many ignorant Seikhs place their firm faith upon it. The Kukas especially believe it firmly. But many learned men do not consider it true and valid. They say that Gooroo Gobind Singh is not the author of this work, for Gooroo did not order to publish the book neither Gooroo Bux Singh Raindar has written it, but he has himself written it out of his own accord. Perhaps some one has written it and has given the name of Gooroo Bux Singh as the author of the work. Some say that the book contains the doctrines of a prophet and description of Seikh religion.

TRANSLATOR'S OPINION.

After a deep research and careful investigation I observe that the book in question was written in the year 1894 Vicramaditya, corresponding to the Christian era 1834, for there are many events and circumstances happened in and about the above year and some years after it. It contains also the prophecies about some distinguished persons who flourished in the above year. Therein such names are mentioned that if any event happens, the coroboration of event or events comes to pass. This will be proved by several tales that are written in the book. The description of the prophecy about Ram Singh Kuka is true and valid, as the following Hindi verse says:—

रिलपुर बीच वाढीसुत होई वर्यो२१लूराज करेगा सोई ॥

Further the book contains the full and accurate decriptions of prophecies which assist others to tell prophecy. In it truth and falsehood are blended together. Religious and secular matters and topics are so described that it is very difficult to separate one from the other. In truth, religious books are thus written as in Mahammedan religion, words of God and prophet are mentioned. But it rests with the author to give a true color to his description according to his experience and knowledge. Learned men make those books easy and plain to understand by various commentaries and notes. Such men generally by the dint of their vast knowledge and experience make the doctrines of religion valid and true according to their own taste and opinion. The accompanying Index will show the true aspect of the book.

SIRDAR ATTAR SINGH,

Chief of Bhadour.

The object of publishing this work and congratulation to the British nation.

Thanks to the Almighty to whose unbounded kindness, we owe the regeneration of this country which the British nation has effected so successfully. The nation in question has created a desire among the people to cultivate learning and has directed their mind towards their own religion. In publishing this work, I pray fervently and sincerely to God, for Her Gracious Majesty the Queen for her disinterested kindness in governing this kingdom and protecting its inhabitants from oppression and misrule. I sincerely believe and wish that this act may be considered as an act of sincere loyalty expressed towards Her Majesty and that this act of sincere loyalty is the chief desire of the Government. It is also the desire of this Government that such a book containing the true account of Seikh religion may be published. I will not withhold myself by publishing this work only, but shall devote my life and labour to publish books containing some of the accounts of Seikh religion which has great affinity with the legislation of the country. Every story of this book contains some accounts of legislation. It is the true cause for the spread of Kuka religion. It is useless to say anything more on the subject. Every one who will read the work, will no doubt, acknowledge the truth of my statement.

SIRDAR ATTAR SINGH,

Chief of Bhadour.

CONTENTS OF SAKHEE.

No. of Page.	No. of Sakhee.	
1		Munglá Chárna or invocation. Preface and introduction to Sakhee or beginning of Uthán; doctrines of Seikh religion, and means how to create faith upon it. The truths of the foretellers and the means by which such truths can be told.
2	1	Bravery of the Seikhs. Birth of the Mussulmans is looked upon with disgrace and the means to create faith upon their birth. Belief of the Seikhs upon their Gooróo; the Mussulman's birth is looked upon by all with censure; hatred towards the Hill tribes; the author's magnanimity of mind and the favour shown to him by God.
6	2	To create a belief that Gooroo is the incarnation of God.
8	3	To create a belief that Gooroo is the prophet.
10	4	Effect of Gooroo's sayings and benedictions upon the minds of his disciples; description of his position as a prophet.
12	5	Interesting tales to create a faith upon religion.
14	6	Interesting tales to create a belief upon the mind of the Seikhs that Gooroo is the incarnation of God.
16	7	Means to form congregation of the Seikhs.
18	8	Necessary rules and actions to follow the religion of the Seikhs; 42 moral instructions i. e. 42 orders. Doctrines of religion; means to form congregation of the Seikhs; to convert Hindoos into Seikhism; to try to spread Seikh religion; description of getting salvation in the next world and of the means of securing other pure terrestrial happiness as laid down in other religion.
24	9	To believe that Gooroo is one of the first prophets; means to form congregation of the Seikhs always near the pond of Muktswar; to declare that the Mussulmans

are the enchanters; to believe the truth, that Sungat Singh will be born.

26 10 Interesting tales; truths of Vedas and Shastras and their revisions, and to believe them according to circumstances and time.

27 11 Praise of singing Gooroo's sayings which is considered as the best way to salvation.

27 12 Interesting tales; to create a belief upon Gooroo; description of the 5 classes of Seikhs.

39 13 Description of the baptism of the Seikhs; to create a belief that Gooroo is a prophet; to encourage Seikh religion; description of the victories of the Seikhs and their old miraculous acts.

33 14 Old tales about the doings and manners of the Seikhs, and their truths; i. e. if Seikh religion becomes weak and corrupted, it should be then considered that such was the order of Gooroo; one tale by which ignorants may believe the truths of Seikh religion; the advent of the English and the French into this country spread of numerous religion and their exposition.

14 15 Prophecy regarding 6000 years of the Kaliyuga i. e. it will end in the year 1900 Vicramaditya. Bad legislation of the country. Birth of Duleep Singh. Prophecied that that he will be good, great, and respectable. Spread of the Englishmen throughout the country. Spread of Seikh religion. To know that Gooroo's words are the words sent by God. Degeneration of the Mussulmans. Victories of the Seikhs and finally their downfall. Again the birth of Gooroo in the A. D. 1743. Advent of the Toorks from Cabul into this country. Devastations prevailed throughout the country. Approach of the English troops from the East. Seikhs joined with the English troops as they had no misunderstanding with each other. Words that create mutual suspicion, and the effect produced by the use of such words; Victory of Duleep Singh. Judicious management of the British nation in governing this kingdom. Birth of Ram Singh

Kuka; there are many prophecies which have produced many dissentions in this country.

39 16 Belief upon Seikh religion. Seikh's examination of the truths and falsities of their own religion. Birth of the Kannaits.

40 17 Tales of Devi's blessings. Best means to form congregation. Means to baptize Seikhs. The bravery and courage of those who embrace Seikh religion. Prophecies in regard to Runjeet Singh.

45 18 Means to form congregation. Animosity with the Hill tribes and the Mussulmans, and its description. Means to strengthen Seikh religion.

46 19 Interesting tales of the treacherous Hill-Tribes.

47 20 Tales to create a faith upon Gooroo by best and reasonable means. To meet death in battle fields ensures a man the enjoyment of paradise.

48 21 Flight of Gooroo from the battle field; this flight on his part was accomplished for the accomplishment of some higher purpose.

49 22 An interesting tale to create a faith upon Gooroo.

50 23 Means to form congregation and to create faith upon Gooroo. Prophecy regarding the forthcoming danger of the Seikhs. Victories of the English. To create a faith upon Dumdum Sahib.

52 24 Strength of the Seikh religion and their Jeehad. Faith upon the religious doctrines promulgated by Gooroo. Description of the bad state of the Mussulmans after their death.

54 25 Classfication of true Seikhs among three caste viz. Jat, Banjara and Rora and their respective descriptions.

57 26 Means to form congregation and to create faith upon Gooroo. Plundering is by far the most laudable profession. Means to infuse strength into Seikh religion.

58 27 Victories of the British soldiers over the Toorks with superior policy. Description of Gooroo's beauty; at last the flight and retreat of the Imperial troops to Delhi. Depression of Aurungzeb.

60 28 Aurungzeb sent a letter to Gooroo to call him. Gooroo sent a reply through his Vakeel. Bravery in the battles and the Vakeel's description of Gooroo's position as a prophet.

63 29 Interesting tales to create a faith upon Gooroo.

64 30 Tales of honesty and praise.

65 31 Moral instructions worth remembering.

66 32 Seikhs converted into Mahammedanism can again be restored to their own religion under the following condition viz. that they should not approach the Mahammedans and should have a faith upon their own religion.

67 33 Tales regarding the praise of the Mahammedan religion and blames and invectives against the Hindoo religion. Gooroo's indifference towards bad actions; means to show the places of worship.

68 34 Means to form congregation of Seikhs.

70 35 Interesting tales as above. Means by which Seikhs can believe upon a prophet. Means to show miracles and the strength of the Seikh religion.

71 36 Battle with the Toorks and the bravery of the Gooroo and the plundering of Khidrabad.

73 37 Battle of Anandpoor and the author's ingenious description of the praise of Runjeet Singh in such a way that his (Runjeet Singh's) blemishes and shortcomings are entirely omitted. To create a faith among the Seikhs, and to examine their conduct. To earn by learning. Prophecy for the advent of the English and the forthcoming contest among the Seikhs, Mussulmans and the English. Such prophecy should be considered true and valid if any of the nations become victorious.

74 38 Plunder of Gooroo's treasure and his flight from the battle field. Such plunder and flight are considered the best policy of Gooroo. To drill and encourage men for battle.

76 39 Treachery of the Hill Tribes, and exposition of the treachery of the Rajpoots.

77 40 Treachery of the Vizier of the Hill Tribes. Miracle. of Gooroo's servants. Prophecy regarding Dalla Chowdry of Sabo.

80 41 A tale regarding Gooroo becoming prophet and an ambassador of God. Prophecy regarding corrupted religion and the conquest of Kandahar. Departure of the English from this country and the advent of the Mussulmans. To omit the description of those difficulties and dangers which Gooroo suffered.

82 42 To create a faith upon Gooroo.

83 43 Praise for keeping Mustaches and beards.

85 44 To show the public the miracles of Gooroo. Description of Gooroo expounding his own religion.

86 45 Prophecy regarding 40 Sakhees i. e. Dalla Barar's tales regarding a faith upon hunting. Description of old miracles.

87 46 A tale regarding the old miracles to show the ignorants the truths of the prophecy, and the manners and customs of the province of Malwa. One paramount means to obey the orders of Gooroo.

88 47 To spread Seikh religion by best means possible.

89 48 Description of Gooroo's miracles and his going to Chimkoer Sahib, and his coming down to Kurukshetra during the occurrence of the eclipse of the sun.

90 49 A tale regarding the love of the Seikhs for their own religion, and the means by which they can maintain themselves; best means to make Sakhee.

92 50 Tales regarding Gooroo becoming prophet, and the spread of the Seikh religion; prophecy regarding the disturbance in the country; prophecy about Futteh Singh.

95 51 Prophecy about Calcutta; mutual battles with the Mahammedans and the English; mutiny among the British troops in the reign of the 20th King of the English nation; Victory of the English troops over the Mussulmans. Rise of the Hindoos and the birth of Ram Singh Kuka. Victory of the Hindoos over the English troops. Duleep Singh becomes King.

97 52 Gooroo entered his Zenanah and the birth of his sons.

98 53 Do. Do. Do.

54 55, 56. As these three Sakhees contain particular description of Gooroo's proceedings in his Zenanah, they are entirely omitted here.

98 57 Gooroo's peace with the Hill Tribes; all Seikhs deserted Gooroo after having left all their claims, except 40 Seikhs who remained with him devotedly.

99 58 Flight of Gooroo towards Malwa, and the manifestation of pride and triumph of the Imperial troops for his precipitate flight. Battle of Ghanoula, and the flight of Gooroo from the field of battle; in this battle only 40 faithful Seikhs who had not deserted Gooroo, fought with the Imperial Force. Defeat of Gooroo. Again by the next day, Gooroo came in contact with the above force at Machhihara, where he, in 1700 Vicramaditya after sustaining defeat, took shelter in the house of a Pathan, by dressing himself in blue clothes, and by sharing the food with him in halves.

102 59 Precipitate flight of Gooroo from Machhihara and the slaughter of Gooroo's sons at Sirhind by the Royal order, and the death of his mother at the same time. Shimir of Dhaliwal caste inhabitant of Kangur served Gooroo in this state of his abject retirement, privately and remained one year with him in the jungle situated near Sirhind, and after the expiration of the above period, he took his departure for Dumdum Sahib, where he heard the death of Aurungzeb.

104 60 Accession of Bahadoor Shah on the throne, and he makes peace with Gooroo and Gooroo's residence in Delhi; before going to Delhi, he went to Pushkur Tirth. Tales about Gooroo becoming Prophet, and his miracles. Gooroo, considering Banda Bairagee his faithful creature, sent him to Punjab to strengthen his own tenets and religion, and to fight for the propogation of his religion. Gooroo next orders Banda to plunder the properties of his enemies which is an ho est and laudable act and lastly ordered that he will be victorious.

108 61 Agreeably to Gooroo's order, Banda brought army from Dukkun and came to Punjab; plundering of Sidhoura, Loodiana, Sirhind and one of the city of Toorks as well as of Doab and his departure to Amritsur. Disunion between the Seikhs and Banda who then at once went down to Sindh where he killed the Seikhs and then became victorious. Advent of the English in the year 1860 and the destruction of the city of Delhie. Seikhs again became victorious and afterwards they became depressed. Mutiny in the year 1899 Vicramaditya and the total depression of Seikh's troops. Prophecy about Moolraj's rebellion at Mooltan.

111 62 Displeasure of the four castes with Gooroo for his introducing new religion. Preparation of weapons of war and their collection. Best means to form congregation. Gooroo's expression of hatred towards the Brahmins. Prophecy about the names of the Seikhs. Curses heaped upon Sodhi castes. Strength of the Seikh religion.

113 63 To create a faith upon the minds of the Seikhs for fighting bravely in battles; prophecy about the victories of the Seikhs. Descriptions of the following nations viz. English and Mharattas and they successively became kings in this country. Prophecy about Dip Singh. General opinions about the disturbance and rebellion in this country.

115 64 Description of Kaliyuga; prophecy about the Mussulmans and the Hindoos; some description about English legislation in this country. Description of the Nepalese becoming king. Avatar Kalki.

118 65 Description of Gooroo becoming Avatar; doctrines of Seikh religion and the moral instructions that contains it.

122 66 Interesting and sound discussions of the author in the Court of Gooroo. Description of salvation.

125 67 Gooroo's faith upon the Brahmins; descriptions of Brahmins' and Seikh religion.

128 68 Prophecy regarding Dip Singh ; several accounts of the faith of the Seikhs upon their Gooroo ; Bravery of the Seikhs. Prophecy regarding rebellion. Rebellion in Kashmeer. Prophecy about Shere Singh, Dhan Singh, Dhogra, Balura Singh, Dho gra that they will be Kings. Prophecy about Seikh religion. To give constant encouragement to the Seikhs for gaining victories over their enemies. Prophecied that Allum Singh will be born in the house of Rangra of Roykote.

130 69 Best means for the improvement of Seikh's religion, and to create a faith upon the minds of the people. Means for Jeehad.

132 70 Best and sound moral instructions of Seikh religion ; animosity of the Seikhs with the Mussulmans and means to form congregation.

134 71 Gooroo gave Yoga instructions in his Zenanah.

136 72 Interesting tales to create a faith upon the minds of the Seikhs.

138 73 Prophecy about the best available means to strengthen and consolidate the religion of the Seikhs. To create bravery in congregation ; a hint from Runjeet Singh about many future occurrences. Description of the miracles of Azizuddeen Fakeer.

140 74 Prophecy about the success and triumph of the religion of the Seikhs ; description of the encouragement given to the Seikhs, and description of Udoy Singh.

143 75 Full and faithful description of Hindoo religion and its union with that of the Seikhs.

146 76 To consider generally the various criticisms of Gooroo as signs of good and laudable actions. Means to become prophet.

148 77 To create a faith upon the minds of the Seikhs upon their Gooroo ; interesting tales.

150 78 Means to spread the religion of Gooroo. To induce the minds of the people to have a firm faith upon their religion ; description of Seikh religion.

154 79 Means to spread the religion of the Seikhs, and to induce men by old ways to have a firm and substantial faith upon religion.

156 80 Do. Do. Do.

158 81 Means for the improvement of Seikh religion ; description of Seikh religion, and interesting tales.

161 82 Moral instructions of the religion of the Seikhs, and the best available means for its improvement.

162 83 Do. Do. Do.

164 84 Description of Hindoo's good actions and their moral instructions.

165 85 Prophecy to create a faith in the mind of Bishumbhur Bania ; prophecy for suggestion to create a rebellion Advent of the English, and the description of the rebellion at Lahore ; description of Sansar Chund and Bharatpoor. Prophecy about Dalal Singh and the original cause of the rebellion at Patil.

170 86 Prophecy about Runjeet Singh's family and his mistress, and a hint for the rebellion in old way.

171 87 Description of the divine favour shown towards the author ; interesting tales and the description of tobacco.

174 88 Best means to spread the use of tobacco among the people, and means to strengthen Seikh religion.

176 89 Prophecy about some of the present occurrences and old events.

178 90 Description of Kaliyuga ; best means to ensure victories to the Seikhs.

180 91 Do. Do. Do.

181 92 Praise of Gooroo's sayings and his words and the miraculous effects produced by them. Gooroo's words and sayings are just like *Tantra.* Best means available to strengthen the tie of congregation.

189 93 Censure of Tobacco.

190 94 Description of leaving tobacco smoking and hatred towards it. The extension of the Mahammedan Empire and the spread of Tobacco.

192 95 Censure of Tobacco. Best instructions for the spread of the religion of the Seikhs, and censure to the Mahammedans.

194 96 Tales regarding the shaving of the heads of the Brahmins. To show the way for the preparation of new Sakhee. Best available means for the learned men to hoist up the standard of rebellion whenever they think proper and good to take possession of countries. Means to spread the religion of the Seikhs.

196 97 Tales of Dadoo Fakeer. Tales of the Hindoos and the Mussulmans. Peace with Bahadoor Shah and Gooroo Gobind, and ultimately Bahadoor Singh's faith upon him.

198 98 Description of the death of Gooroo who died as a prophet, to believe that Gooroo was an incarnation of God.

200 99 Do. Do. Do.

02 100 Prophecy about the forthcoming rebellion, description of the income of Ahmud Shah Kabuli; description of Runjeet Singh and the miracles of the Gooroo; various benefits and blessings which the offsprings of the author derived for spreading this book throughout the length and breadth of the country.

Conclusion.

RAM.

"MUNGLA CHURN" OR PREFACE.

SAHIB SINGH the writer of the following pages commences his work after reseating to the protection of the lotus like feet of those Gooroos whose blessed names are below mentioned.

(1) The blessed faced Baba Nanuk, Gooroo Angud, Gooroo Amer Dass, Gooroo Ram Dass, Gooroo Argun, Gooroo Hargobind, the 9 of good qualities, Gooroo Har Rai, and Gooroo Har Kishen worthy of being worshipped, Gooroo Teg Bhadar, the most patient, and Gooroo Gobind Sing like a lion to his deer-like enemies and praised by Toorks.[1]

Sahib Singh writes a book of the Gooroo's words as heard from Goorbux Singh who was also called Ram Kour one of the descendants of Boodha, the servant of Gooroo and house of comfort who always attended to the 10th Gooroo[2] and always acted according to his orders the Gooroo's[3] saying was that in order to teach the right wisdom and policy, it is necessary that the teacher and pupil must be right minded men and the way they follow must be right. The religion of Seikhs spread just in the manner as the Gooroo had predicted. All the Sungut[4] asked Goor Bux Singh about the life accounts and the predictions of the Gooroo and the writer being one of the assembly, writes as he heard at that time. The Goor Bux Sing recollected from his grand father Boodha what

---

[1] Mahammedans.

[2] Gooroo Gobind Sing.

[3] The Gooroo always denote Gooroo Gobind Sing in this book.

[4] A body of the true followers of Georoo Gobind Sing.

he related at that time. The subject related at that occasion was easy and was such as could fulfil the desires of the public. This collection of Gooroo's words is fitted to shower blessings on the Seikhs who may believe in it with love. Mathra Misir the old attendant of the Gooroo understanding the private wishes of the Gooroo asked various questions about the futurity and the Gooroo revealed to him in the manner. The Kirshen had done to the Oodroh. One Ram Dass collected those sweet Sakhees just as the Gooroo had spoken. This book is written in singh a walokun style, that is a style in which a subject is more than once repeated in order to complete it details.

SAKHEE FIRST.

The city of Patna is the birth place of Gooroo Gobind Sing who was the 10th Gooroo. Sahib Singh writes true words of the Gooroo in the presence of Ram Kour as correctly and exactly as his abilities allow. The Gooroo had revealed this on Thursday 2nd Baisakh sub 1791, a month of the leap year. All the assembly of the Seikhs considered and found Sahib Sing worthy of writing Sakhee. Any omission or mistake that may be discovered in this should be corrected by none but one who may have been a constant attendant of the Gooroo, any other person trying to correct it will be drowned in trouble and difficulty.

The Gooroo made a joke with Goor Bux Singh, and said well have you done! Four, Four, and Four, Four and Five, Five, is your work, these are the only person who could relate of four Beds, of four[1] motives of four yogs, and of four sources[2] of creation. Of five places from which letters are uttered and of five sorts of letters. The

---

[1] Four motives are Faith Wealth, Enjoyment, Salvation.

[2] The four sources of creation believed by Hindoo Philosophers are Egg, Womb, Sweat and Earth.

hairs, all over the body and the nice big knot of hairs on the head is the cloak granted by Bhawanee,[1] to all the Seikhs.

The Gooroo inculcated to his Seikhs that morning is the best time for worship and sacred ablutions, do not tremble: It is horse and elephant's habit to bathe after eating.

On one occasion, all the Khalsa[2] said, O! Gooroo, the power of "Moghuls" and "Pathans" has greatly increased give us permission to fight and suppress it. The Gooroo in reply said, once god of death avowed that he would kill no creature, the people increased in great number, and fear of death vanished, the world became awfully crowded, the people forgot their religious worships and fell to meanness seeing this, gods went and complained before "Brahma," saying, that the Digpals[3] were appointed by your order as Governors on the eight sides of the world, the mad people used to give us bali.[4] They have now ceased to do it, because the God of death has ceased to send death over them and has engaged himself in devotions. Brahma said such is the will of Almighty God, He is at liberty to do or not to do, He is the master of his own will. You should all go to your own places. So all the gods went to their respective residences. In the mean while, the time of the vow of god of death was at end, he saw the people increased to an enormous crowd and was wavering like a heavey-laden boat, he was filled with anger and remembered Rooder[5] and by the effect of this, mankind began to be reduced to ashes. Some were destroyed by fire, some by wind, and some by water. The famine appeared, the

---

1 A famous Goddess in Hindoo Mythology.

2 The whole body of Seikhs.

3 Police officers of gods.

4 Pieces of bread offered to gods as sacred offerings.

5 One of the Hindoo Trinity who is believed to be the representative of the destroying power of God.

remaining men fled away and took refuge in the city of "Julal" "Gundhurb," i. e. the city of "Kundhar." These persons began to multiply in that city. In the Mahabharath-war, greater number of these were killed and few were saved. These remaining persons broke up their castes and began to intermarry without scruple.

The Governor of that city in those days was "Momun Shurf," he went one day in a Garden and enticed away the women of that nation and took them to his house. The women who insisted to defend their chastity by saying that they would die, were promised to be made chiefs: These women became at last his wives and children were born from them. One of them was the daughter of Viddya Dhur Pathuk" a Brahmin. From her, Potul Khan Pathan was born. Mogul "Mongul Beg" was born from Moodguli Brahmine and Sekh Summon was born from the danghter of Sekhra Sukhawut, and a son was born from Sugatee, whom Momun Shurf asked, who she was, and learning she was the daughter of Shoojat Rai, his son, felt ashamed, Shooját Rai was the son of Momun Shurf and born from one of his principal and legally married wives and had been previously banished from his country. Momun Shurf, fearing from this horrible sin, took himself to the refuge of Hidajut Shurf devotee and began to serve him. When many days were passed the devotee said to Momun Shurf do not fear, and be content with the will of God, the children of this Sagatee will be called Syads and will assist your chidren in the time of difficulty. Engage yourself in forty day's devotions, and you will undoubtedly be cleared from sin.

The Gooroo then said, O my Seikhs! these men had fled there from the god of death, and were at last killed by "Arjun"[1] and "Bheem" Pandoos. The god of death was enraged on that nation. We will kill the four

[1] The famous heroes of Mahabharath.

Shaikhs[1] with the assistance of our followers, who increase as rapidly as millions of Brahama and Shiva are produced from the Almighty God. The Seikhs then asked, O true King! will any one be saved or not, the Gooroo replied it is ordained that none will remain out of them, the Khalsa will kill them all, but many others who having seen them had left their own faith and had joined with them, will be saved. Three days after this, the Gooroo took up his bow and going out in plains drew it, when a sound was heard from heaven, saying, "O Gooroo! save us from Mountains and Forests." The Gooroo then proceeded on the back of blue horse for gaming, and was met with Rajas Rulia Chund and Alum Chund, who with an army came upon the Gooroo, with the intention of fighting and wanted to show their power and bravery. The Gooroo made his horse run towards the east for there were few Seikhs with him. In the meanwhile the Mountaineers arrived and the Seikhs began to fight with them. A bloody battle ensued. The Seikhs looked back and saw that the Gooroo was not there. They thought among themselves that the Gooroo left them alone, and ran after him and began to cry out O! Gooroo save us, for we are your disciples. A forest does not look well without lion. The Gooroo replied, be of good faith and continue to read my words, you yourself will be lion and Forest, Divine service is the true and excellent task. Having said this, he discharged five arrows by the effect of which Seikh armies appeared on all four sides, the battle began to rage, the Gooroo standing by "Karounda Tree" inspected the battle. The Khalsa by power of the Gooroo defeated the Mountaineers, who fled away. I (Goor Bux Singh) then trembled, O! Sahib Singh, the Gooroo told me, "O! Goor Bux Singh, I will leave you and go to heavens just as Krishna had done with Ooddhoo, fear not, fear not,—I then wept, the Gooroo said Khalsa is returning after defeating Mountaineers. In the mean-

[1] The principal man of that nation.

while Khalsa arrived, the heavenly armies vanished. The Gooroo looked with the eyes of kindness over them and said the Mountaineers are Hindoos. The Khalsa replied Mountaineers are our food like wild beasts. The Gooroo repeated 3 times, that Mountaineers are proud of their royal power, and do not believe in the fate ordained by God, who has well acted in creating the 3rd Nation, the Khalsa. Your sorrows will vanish away. One who has created has destroyed. The Khalsa upon hearing this were filled with pleasure and rejoiced. This Sakhee is finished. Mahan Singh gave full account of the battle.

SAKHEE SECOND.

One day Purmanund Wuzeer met the Gooroo in Court hall with great love. The hall was filled with a large number of wise men and every one was speaking of his religion. One of them Mudan Dass Bairagee said O! Gooroo the Karah Prashad is a special food of "Hunooman" and "Devi," why did Baba Nanuk select it for himself, probably because he was an old man, and it being an easy smooth and delicious food suited him well. The Gooroo said a similar question was once put to Baba Nanuk by "Sain Dass Bairagee" and Baba Nanuk had replied him as follows:—It had once gone to Utra Khund and it was the first occasion on which I had set on my tour after retirement, I arrived on Himnoor Hills and, met several Sidh and Naths there, who accosted me (Baba Nanuk) by saying Ades! Ades! I said Ades to Almighty God! Sidhs requested me to give them a feast I told them wait, God will give you a feast and thus promising to give them a feast I went off and left Bhai Murdana and Bhai Bala there. As I was going to the Ganges bank "Vishnu" appeared to me in the shape of a Sidh and gave me sand, which afterwards turned into sugar, on proceeding further, Brahama met me likewise in the shape of a Sidh and gave me water which afterwards turned into Ghee, in the same manner I was met with Mahadeva in the shape of Sidh, who gave me some ash, which afterwards turned into wheat-flour. Many other Rikhs met and gave me ingredients such as black pepper, and Chironji[1] and then disappeared from sight. I returned and ordered Bala to distribute food, which I put behind a large flat piece of stone. When I had gone to Ganges banks, the assembly of Sidhs thought in their mind that I had gone to procure some fruits for them and they in order to make a jest with me, turned themselves in the shape of very old men, saying to themselves, that they will decline to eat fruits on the pretence of their being very old and having no teeth and that they will ask for a smooth food, suitable to their age, which, I will be unable to give. All this they did to try me and to see whether I could work miracles. I distributed "Karah Prasad" to them which was miraculously prepared. They were pleased and satisfied by eating it, and told me, excellent! excellent! this food is, you should also eat it. I also ate it and told them O! Sidhs, this my little quantity of food is sacred. By eating this, men will be purified and will become stronger and abler in applying themselves to devotion, divine meditations and fastings, and their minds will be pleased. Sidhs called me blessed and said for preparing this food, "Vishnu" had supplied you with sugar "Mahadeva" with wheat flour and "Brahama" with Ghee Rikhs with fruits and "Shree Bhawanee" with cloth of leaves. How can we fight with one who is protected by God. Be kind to us, your food is worthy of being enjoyed by Devtas and any person using it with love in the days of Kaliyug will have a great share of sacred virtues and will be saved from sin. I then said that Karah mixed with *Aniseseed* will be peculiar to Hunooman and Karah mixed with Cocoanut will be peculiar to Devi, and Karah

[1] Nuts of Chironjia Sapida.

mixed with ingredients *i. e.* pepper chironji &c., will be special to Gooroo (myself) but this karah must be "Tirbhawali-walla,"[1] if it be otherwise, it will not be accepted by Gooroo. The Sidhs then disappeared. Sakhee 2nd finished.

SAKHEE THIRD.

At a certain time Sungut assembled to obtain the blessings of seeing the sacred face of the Gooroo, and were praising the blessings resulting from their being in Gooroo's attendance. The Gooroo appeared so magnificent as he was Komer,[2] sitting dressed in splendid garment and wearing a precious shawl. The Gooroo ordered that the whole assembly of male and female Seikhs be prevented from going away to their houses. The assembly was, therefore, prevented for three days, after which they felt it very inconvenient to remain there as it was long since they had been absent from their respective private businesses and now wanted to go home. They wanted to obtain a speedy permission for going, but the Gooroo being engaged in hearing sacred songs, no one could dare to ask for the permission. One of the assembly, who was a Seikh of Malwa country contrived a plan for getting rid of such prevention and played the following trick. He prepared a coffin after Hindoo fashion and made a living man to lie in it like a dead body carried it with the procession mourning and singing this verse "disciples true love is completed and come to an end," by the way where the Gooroo held his durbar. By the order of the Gooroo a servant enquired and informed the Gooroo that a Seikh had died. The Gooroo ordered the coffin to be brought in, and it was done so. The procession accompanying the

---

[1] Having sugar, ghee and wheat-flour of equal weight.

[2] The God of wealth.

dead also came in, some of them were weeping and some singing songs of sorrow. The Gooroo stopped the Seikh women from crying. In the meantime, when four ghurees had passed, the Gooroo spoke to the Ardasia and said, O! my Seikh brother, it is very difficult to become a true Seikh, but there is a large number of such persons who appear like Seikhs in their forms. The person who has true faith in the Gooroo is very rare, what is the advantage of singing sacred songs and weeping with false love? If it be said that weeping pleases the Gooroo then the whole village weep on dead corps. If it be said that sacred songs please God, then parrots and pigeons also sing sweetly. If it be said that bathing pleases God, then frogs always live in water. If it be said that silence pleases the God, then trees are always silent. If it be said the living of forests pleases the God then, deers &c. always live in forests.

Consequently without a little of faith and true love, Seikhs, Pundit and Singers remain deprived. The Ardasia said, O! true King, sacred sight of the Gooroo saves the Seikhs from evil and the present assembly are enjoying your sacred sight and are singing songs of sacred love. Therefore they will certainly be saved. The Gooroo replied that one who is positive in his own opinion loses, and one, who believes in Gooroo's words, gains. All the people enjoy sun's sight, but this does not clear them from their sins and they consequently go to hell. In this world, there is no god like water, but still in bathing in a Teeruth sacred love is the principal thing. The moon, stars, wind, and Indra's sight does not give salvation. All men and women are filled with bashfulness if they have faith, they will certainly pass over to heaven. The Gooroo then said to Ardasia if you wish to see the "Tamasha"[1] bring the burning piece of wood and put it under the

[1] Fun.

coffin. It was done so. As soon as the heat of fire reached the dead, he startled and throwing aside the shawl with which he was covered ran out of the coffin. All the Sungut were put to astonishment and the persons of the family of the dead felt ashamed. The Gooroo told them, brethren, by your sacred love and through the result of your sacred songs the dead has fled to heavens with his body. The Seikhs bowed down and said O! true king, you only know your things. The Gooroo then said O my Seikhs if you would have succeeded in deceiving me, you should have said to your family persons in your home, that Gooroo is just like other men, and thus you should have lost your faith in me. The Gooroo then looked towards the Seikhs and said, O! my Seikhs, Baba Nanuk's saying is this. Gooroo joins the separated persons and is able to forgive all. May He, the Forgiver, forgive all and, O! Nanuk, may he make us cross safely the ocean of the miseries and temptations of this world. The Gooroo then permitted the Sungut to go to their houses. Here ends the 3rd Sakhee.

SAKHEE FOURTH.

The Gooroo was once present in his Sungut who were not yet satisfied with seeing the Gooroo. A Seikh and his wife begged before the Gooroo and said, O! true King, by your favour we have a son, who has retired from family, and speaks roughly and lovelessly with his wife, who is the daughter of a respectable household, we are much in pain on account of his this sort of conduct, when we admonish him, he says that he would leave us and going to strange country would become a Fukeer.[1] He ordered him to be brought in presence and it was done so. The young Seikh stood with folded hands before the Gooroo, who asked

[1] A retired devotee.

him, O brother, your parents say that you have retired from the world, how this desire of retirement is produced in your heart, whose disciple are you, what is your name and what profession you prefer, speak the truth, you appear to be 18 years of age and the people do not wish to leave the enjoyments till the old age, you are very fortunate, we wished for the blessings of your Durshun (sight) and consequently have called you here. The young Seikh replied O! true King why are you joking with me. I am a creature of the ocean-like world and will pass over this ocean through the effects of your Durshun (sight) you knowing all secrets, still ask me, my name is Nund Singh and am Seikh of the Gooroo, desire of retirement has sprung out of Gooroo's words, for it is said that whoever will resort to Gooroo's protection, whether he be a boy or an old man, will be saved as when a person rides on a boat he crosses the river safely. O true king, my parents taught me Gooroo's words, which I learnt by heart. The love of reading was produced in my heart and I once contemplated on a verse of "Anundjee," which means this: "All the relations, whom you seest will not go with you, why then do you give your heart to such." The meanings of this verse are set in my heart and this has produced a desire of retirement. I have left my family and the world appears to me nothing but vanity, and dispersing like a cloud, you can distinguish if there is any other fault in me. I have forgotten eating, drinking, laughing &c. and am come to your protection. This is the effect of your words. The Gooroo then addressed his parents and said, do not be superstitious, your son is not effected by Ghosts, do not bother him, I will admonish him myself, and I have granted you another son, which will shortly be born. Leave this young Seikh with me, his wife will remain happy, and he himself will become a family-man. The parents of the young Seikh bowed before the Gooroo and went their way. The young Seikh remained with the Gooroo and made it his constant habit to sit before the Gooroo with folded hands. Here ends the 4th Sakhee.

SAKHEE FIFTH.

The Gooroo one day said to the young Seikh, Nund Singh, O young brother I am going to relate a story before you, listen it with attention and then you can do whatever you like. "There was a certain devotee living in a Forest, who was of a contented mind and would not move out of his cottage. In the vicinity of this cottage there was a village, the inhabitants of which used to bring him little or more .every sorts of sweet or sour things, such as grain, flour, curd, vegetable, milk &c. and he used to accept and enjoy it as sent by God, and remained always enjoyed in yog[1] exercises, and having had a full understanding of the 12 sorts of Anáhud sound closely shut his mind from wandering towards worldly objects. The name of the devotee as used by the villagers was "Jawala." On one occasion he could get no food for seven days so he thought that the Almighty God was displeased with him for not using his limbs in procuring his livelihood, the purpose for which they were given him. He thought it proper to go to city, and to procure something by way of "Durshun Bhiksha" the gods will be displeased to give me in laziness. Having thought this he prepared himself for going to the village and took with himself, his stick, rind of gourd, quilt of rags, small carpet of poa and string of beads, the marks of devotional life, for without such marks it is not good to go to the house of worldly-men. If a devotee going to the house of a citizen without marks may be mistreated by him, he the citizen can not be held guilty of such ill-treatment. It is not good for a Sadhoo to go for begging twice in a day and to change his devotional marks. He should always accept "Doodh-bhiksha,"

[1] Devotional exercises.

viz., a thing which the giver may give of his own free will. For a devotee should not stop for a long time at one place and should not take food prepared by fire for it becomes unholy, if it be touched by women or children, whosoever eats food prepared by another is not a true devotee, for, it it is said that a person is deprived of his sacred love towards God, if he eats the food prepared by one of whose manner of living and of his spiritual guide nothing be known. Having considered on these things, the devotee went to the village. In the village, a rich banker had given a great religious feast to Brahmins and poor, and the people were crowded at his door, and he was engaged in feeding every one of them. This devotee also went and stood before his door till evening, but no one took notice of him nor gave any food to him. He was at last disappointed and went back to his house. When it was midnight two angels of "Vishnu" god with burning torches in their hands came to his house and told him, O devotee! we are sent by god to burn the house of that rich banker who has given a feast to-day, for he did not pay due regard to you, and let you return hungry to your house. He even did not pay respect to devotional marks and is therefore a great sinner. Come now with us and show us his house. The devotee accompanïed them and asking a torch from them began to burn them with it. The angels fled. The devotee then said, the banker gave food to every one, he had no enmity with me he should have also given me food if God had wished it. He has no power. Providence is the secret agent of all and He, in fact, distributes every thing. He is the Master of the world, we all are subject to His power and I pay compliments to him. Beware, not to do this again. Both angels then bowed before the devotee and presenting themselves before Vishnu god said, O great King! that devotee is one who loved in true business, the Vishnu then sent heavenly chariots and called the devotee above in the heaven.

The Gooroo after repeating this story told the Seikh youth O young brother, understand the true sense of this narrative. What can the poor creatures do, if the God himself forget them. Hear and be wise, if you want to become a retired man, you should try to make yourself as strict as that devotee.

SAKHEE SIXTH.

The Gooroo continued to speak and said O Young Seikh, Baba Nanuk says, "The nose-string of the bull is in the hands of his owner, who can carry him wherever he likes. Likewise the good or bad acts of this man drive him to whatever befalls him; man should be contended with his will. He himself is the slate, the pen, and the writer, and there is no one beside Him. This is the "truth." The Gooroo then said O young brother, if you ever become a house-hold, you should behave as pigeons did in the following story. In a forest there was a tree of thick shade, on which a nest was built by a pair of pigeons who had also their young ones with them. Once a fowler went out with his net to kill birds. Being overtaken by heavy storm and shivering with cold, took refuge under that tree. He could not trace his way home and being reduced extremely by hunger and terror intended to pass the night there. The pigeon seeing that man in such reduced circumstances, addressed his wife, saying O my best half, we are house-holders and this man in such a reduced condition has come to our house. Our duty is to feed him and to provide for his convenience. We have no hands but God has given us a bill. Let us try to provide for the convenience of this man, for everything is done with exertion. Wealth is obtained by exertions, as wind is procured by fan. Saying this he fled to a goat-farm and catching a burning piece of goat-dung, cast it before the man with the dry straw and chaff off his nest. The man seeing fire and dry straw before him, collected dry fuel which were plenty in that place and making a good fire warmed himself. The pigeon then said to his wife, that in order to remedy the hunger of that man, he would make himself his prey, and that she should take care of the young ones, but the female did not accept it and said she would die first to become a food for the guest. For she said she would be able to do nothing after him. Woman is a filthy creature and is of no use without man, who is the contributor of ease. The pigeon said a man without woman is like a wall of sand. The man is a hero of outward businesses and feels much difficulty in conducting homely business. While this conversation was going on, the female pigeon fell in the burning fire and was roasted. The fowler finding a roasted prey before him ate it. After this the pigeon thought that the fowler must be still hungry for the quantity that a man daily consumes, is 3 Seers, how could this man have been satisfied with one pigeon's flesh, and it is said in the "Veda" one who gives his guest half the quantity of food that is necessary to feed him, goes to hell. Thinking this, threw himself in the fire. The fowler seeing this was filled with mercy and said alas! such a Godly being has died merely for the sake of the feeding me. I am a great sinner and heavy sin is attached to me. I will now give up myself wholly to devotion whether my life remains or not. Having said this, he began to weep with affection. In the meantime angels arrived with heavenly chariots, and took the fowler and all the family of pigeons to the heaven. O young brother, the Gooroo said, these are the two ways of leading life, which of these do you prefer. Besides, there are many ways by which Sadhs and worldly men are ruining themselves. O young Seikh, the Kubeer devotee who is the chief of four yogs, and who was both devotee and family man, has said that a man should complete his life in the manner he has begun. This is more valuable than diamond and thousands of precious stones. The young Seikh said, O Gooroo I obey you, and am your disciple and will be able to lead a family life, but I have, little or more, a desire for retirement, and my limbs are weak, but I will serve the body of Seikhs as much as I can. The Gooroo laughing said, continue to serve the Gooroo, who will take a portion of your burden. O young Seikh, in previous birth you were a servant of my horse and your name was Mundoo. On that occasion, in night time, I had told you to go and look after my horse, you falsely said, you had supplied my horse with plenty of grass and grain, I at that time told you, O Sluggish, how will you be able to carry on your household business; you hearing this exclaimed, "The Gooroo has killed a poor man!" I having heard your voice was moved with compassion and promised to protect you. At that time in the last Kaliyug, I had born to defend faith by the will of God, and had then obtained the dignity of Gooroosbip through heavy devotions. Remain, your household affairs will be well fared by the favor of Gooroo. The young Seikh then consented to live with his family and began to serve the Gooroo. Here ends the 6th Sakhee.

SAKHEE SEVENTH.

Once in the month of Bhado, the raining season, when it was night, the Gooroo went on the top of his house to sleep. There was a certain servant of the Gooroo called Lahoura Singh, who owed a certain sum of money to a banker called Malla Singh, who was now in reduced circumstances, but was possessed of modesty, Malla Singh asked every day for the payment of debt due by Lahoura Singh, but Lahoura Singh took no notice of it and evaded him. One night Malla Singh was induced by his wife and being much vexed, went to Lahoura Singh's house and quarrelled with him, Lahoura Singh said, it is not a matter of anxiety, if a Seikh has consumed another Seikh's property. Gooroo has allowed every one to eat, drink, and be merry, and every one gets as is allotted to him by God. Hearing this Malla Singh said to not become violent, those who act falsely will be punished in the next world, and will be beaten before the Yama (the Judge of the deceased ones). They will then weep and repent. The debtor then said no one will call for account when the Gooroo will forgive. The Gooroo, as he was lying down in bed on the top of his house, heard this conversation (for that house of Lahoura Singh was closed to Gooroo's house) and thought himself that my Seikh has made himself positive on wrong points and has thrown his burden upon the Gooroo. He has learnt the verse, but has acted very little upon it. The Gooroo then spoke out and gave the following three answers to Lahoura Singh's remarks.

1. A man eating out of his brother's pocket should not become his enemy, but should remain under the command of his brother.

2. The Gooroo makes a man reap according to his own acts.

3. Baba Nanuk has said that another man's due is like cow-flesh to Hindoos and like hog-flesh to Mahammedan.

Gooroo and Peer assist only to that man who does not procure his livelihood by unlawful means. Lahoura Singh hearing this, was pressed, and paid off his debt on the following morning, after which he went to the Gooroo and having made a bow before him said, a covetous and debauched Seikh becomes separate from the Gooroo but the Gooroo forgives him and calls him near. The Gooroo then said those orders of Gooroo which are according to "Veda" and Dhurma's precepts are true. Here ends the 7th Sakhee, and the 8th relates of the duties of a Seikh.

SAKHEE EIGHTH.

O Seikh of Gooroo, hear the salvation book of the Gooroo. Whoever will not act according to the precepts of the Gooroo, will be a false disguiser. The following are the precepts of the Gooroo to his Seikhs:—

1 A Seikh should not contract debt, but if he does he should repay it with pleasure.

2 He should keep his wife happy and should direct her to good way.

3 He should not speak a lie, nor hear it, nor love it

4 He should earn the truth, should keep the true company, should nourish the true love, should become a true merchant, a true hero, a true Pundit, a true adviser, a true cultivator, a man of true profession, should entertain the love of true knowledge.

5 He should not eat food, a part of which has been eaten by another.

6 He should not be slave of money.

7 He should first distribute a share of his food to those who are present on that occasion, and then eat it himself.

8 He should not eat nor sleep bare-headed.

9 He should repeat the name of Gooroo before he begins to eat.

10 He should read jupjee[1] before he takes meals.

11 He should not see naked women.

12 He should not contemplate of women.

13 He should not touch another man's property and the ass.

---

[1] A sacred treatise of Seikhs, composed by Baba Nanuk which is in the beginning of "Adigrunth."

14 He should keep himself far from mean fellows.

15 He should not eat flesh of the animal or bird slaughtered by Mahammedans.

16 He should not eat flesh of the bred[1] swine.

17 He should not drink wine.

18 He should remain exalted in mind.

19 He should wash his hands after making water.

20 He should wash his hands and feet with dust and water, after easing himself.

21 He should bathe with cold water as early as three o'clock in the morning. Gooroo Gobind Singh says, that such a person will be saved from the punishment of Yama.[2]

22 He should keep himself aloof from the world though always engaged in business.

23 He should not wear clothes dyed with Indian Saffron.

24 He should not beautify or blacken the eyes with antimony in the day time.

25 He should not become naked.

26 After repeating the name of God he should read Arta[3], for, by so doing the Gooroo annihilates poverty.

27 He should take Pauhul[4] and should behave as directed in the "Grunth."

28 He should serve his own religion and should not be led astray by the doctrines of other religions.

29 He should eat in the house of fellow-Seikhs.

30. He should marry his daughter with a Seikh.

---

[1] i. e. Village swine as distinct from wild-swine.

[2] The Judge of the deceased.

[3]

[4] Baptism of the Seikh religion.

31. He should discharge the duties prescribed in the Vedas with freedom.[1]

32. He should keep aside his wife and son from bad company.

33. He should read Gooroo's Munter[2] and should perform the household business incessantly.

34. He should not enjoy the money or any other thing offered to gods.

35. He should eat Karah every day, and should eat the leavings of food offered to Gooroo. He should also eat Gooroo's Prashad, which may be given to him by the Ardasia.[3]

36. The Ardasia should distribute the Gooroo's pershad equally. Envious feelings towards the distribution of Prashad creates disunion. Whoever is covetous in obtaining Pershad, i. e. tries to obtain greater portion by hypocrisy, theft &c., he should be liable to Yama's punishment. The Pershad obtained by deceit, causes destruction, sickness, sorrow and adversity.

37. A Seikh when taking his meals, should not stand nor leave his dish, but if he leaves it, he should not again begin to eat out of the same; whosoever obeys this precept, will be happy, rich, and in the protection of the Gooroo.

38. He should save himself from a Mahammedan man or woman.

39. He should not hate a Seikh.

40. He should eat from and give food to his fellow-Sheik, no matter if he belongs to any of the four Hindoo castes.

---

[1] That as considering himself free from all bonds. He should keep the ceremonies of Vedas for the sake of consistency in society.

[2] Verses taught by the Gooroo.

[3] A servant of Gooroo's shrine.

41. He should not adopt the doctrines of disguisers.[1]

42. He should not eat of the food offered to Teetla goddess.

43. He should not eat the food over which the words of Mahammedan Kulwa are read.

44. He should consider Mahammedans as an illness.

44. *a.* He should forsake a false Brahman, a false Seikh and a widow woman.

44. *b.* He should live with pride.

45. He should not become a slave of a prostitute.

46. He should prepare "Tirbhamla Kharah" with pure and clean hands and after he has well purified himself by bathing &c., then he should offer this Karah to the Gooroo, but at the time of performing the ceremony of offerings he should not become naked. For by so doing he can obtain his desire. In this world his faith is proved and in the next he will obtain rest.

47. Whosoever will call a Seikh with half name, that foolish man will be liable to fine.

48 Whosoever will be obstinate like Mahammedans, will be made to live in hell.

49. A Seikh should not enjoy woman, except one who is married[1] to him by Anund ceremony; whoever does not behave according to this precept, hear, O Seikh I tell you emphatically, he will not be my Seikh.

50. A Seikh should not sleep at the time of sunset and sun rise.

51. He should be far from unclean and impure things, and food of which a portion has been eaten by

---

[1] Is meant by various classes of Hindoo Faqueers.

[2] A special marriage-ceremony of Seikhs, which is nearly as simple as Christian marriage ceremony.

another; such a man and worthy of living with the Gooroo and lives in the presence of Devtas, and gods.

52. He should not eat with loose flowing hairs and should tie his hairs in knot at the time of eating.

53. He should give tenth part of his earnings for religious purposes and enjoy the remainder himself.

54. He should clean his teeth with small stick cut out of the branches of trees and then bathe and repeat Gooroo's verses early in the morning, and should pay compliments to his fellow Seikhs.

55. He should intermarry in Seikh families, and should not marry a daughter of the house who are of the Got with his paternal or maternal families. Out of such marriage, the Gooroo will grant good children.

56. He should not always weep for the deceased relative of a Seikh, he should prepare Karah, read the Anund verses and give up all mournings. Nor should women continue in long mournings. He should cause the sacred songs of Gooroo to be sung and should feed the assembly of devotees, Brahmins and Seikhs and should give them some cash also. At the same time he should not forsake the Bed ceremonies and should burn the dead and perform the funeral obsequies according to the sacred Book of Bed.

57. One who shaves the long hairs of his head, which is a mark of the Gooroo, is faithless, and one who causes the heads of his son or brethren to be shaved, will suffer the pains of Yamraj and will become a wretched Ghost. No one should make a relation with such a person nor eat together with him. Whoever nourishes such a person, is a sinner. This is a positive order of the Gooroo Gobind Singh.

58. Whosoever learns Persian language for the sake

of earning his livelihood and trusts in the friendships of a Mahammedan is rebellious.

59. On the occasion of a son's birth, marriage, or death, he should pay Tankhwah[1] and cause his irregularities to be forgiven.

60. That Seikh who does not eat food of a Moua[2] is a special favorite of the Gooroo.

61. A Seikh, whose Pouhal ceremony is performed, should not worship a stone nor drink water by which a stone is washed.

62. Whoever is free from the ceremonies of Burns and Ashrums, is a trade Seikh in this world.

63. There are numerous duties, such as duties towards gods, duties towards father and those towards grandfather, but a Seikh should care to discharge none but those towards the Gooroo.

64. A Seikh should not vex the following persons, *viz.*, the descendants of the Gooroo, one who is a great man according to Vedas, a person wholly devoted to God, a generous man, a King or Chief or Brahman.

The following persons feel themselves miserable and weep *viz.*, one who reads Veda, but is not acquainted with its secrets, a sinner, one cursed by the Gooroo, one who is ill of a very long disease.

Whoever has come to my house, *i. e.* has accepted my religion, he should love the words of Gooroo, should hear the Gooroo's precepts and adopt them. He should live clever and clean.

I will forgive such a person and will make him get

---

[1] A fine among Seikhs paid to the servants of Gooroo's shrine in order to have the irregularities committed in observing Seikh ceremonies, forgiven.

[2] Moua, a person not belonging to Seikh religion and not wearing long hairs or his head.

over this world. I will give him my own position. This position cannot be measured even by Sunkra Charya, Dutta Treh, Ramanooj, Goorukh and Mahammed. As a field flourishes by rain, so will the Dhurma[1] flourish in the presence of the Gooroo. The Gooroo ordered that whoever will read this Mokut Nama,[2] and will bathe in the sacred reservoir of Mokutsur, will be freed from evil acts and after death will go to Gooroo's house. The Gooroo, then said, hear O young Seikh the fruit of hearing these 42 verses of precepts which I have related to you is, that a man is saved from the pains of 84 Lakhs of births, as easily and simply as a shut up air flies. The Gooroo then said, enough, blessed art thou O young Seikh live like a true Seikh and do not hear the world.

Here ends the 8th Sakhee.

SAKHEE NINTH.

One day, the Gooroo had just risen from his bed when a naked Seikh of exhausted breath came running alone before the Gooroo, who asked him what is the matter ? Is it all well ? The Seikh after bending his head before the Gooroo, replied, O true king I am a Bunjora[3] Seikh and have seen a very strange thing, i. e. a Mahammedan has egaged the affections of a Seikh woman who is enchanted in such a way that she always speaks in his favor, and says that she will no longer remain in Seikhsim. The Gooroo said, her husband must be a pupil of Mahammedan Peers[4] and should have been accustomed to eat Sheernee.[5] The Seikh begged, "forgive O' Gooroo, she is my sister's daughter, I and my sister are believers of Seikhism from

---

[1] Dhurm, religious virtues.

[2] A Treatise of Salvation i. e. this Chapter of precepts.

[3] A Got or subdivision of the caste of Seikhs.

[4] Mohammedan Demi-prophet.

[5] Sweatmeat offered to Peers.

the very beginning, and her maternal and paternal families are all true Seikhs. The Gooroo said, make her bathe in the sacred reservoir of Mookutsur, for she will thus be saved from evil manners; recite "Mookutnama"[1] to her and read Jupjee[1] 40 times to her and writing 8 letters of the phrase "Wah[2] Gooroo Jee Sahai" on a paper, bind it around her neck or put it in the hairs of her head on the 1st Sunday of the new moon. By doing this, she will become better and will get rid of the effects of Ghosts. O brother, believe in Seikhism, this is good. Mere outward forms are not good. Gooroo loves true belief only and is not ambitious of money and offerings. Whosoever will forgive a sinner of Seikhism for the sake of money, will be a thief before the Gooroo. His Seikhism will not be accepted by the Gooroo. The Seikh then bowed his head and went away. The Gooroo's order was carried out and the Seikh woman became amended.

Once the Gooroo went to her house in the village of "Joomman Khera." She bent her head before the Gooroo and said, O Gooroo I was enchanted by a Mahammedan and am now repenting. The Gooroo said, O Seikh woman, no one becomes polluted without sexual intercourse. We should not trust in the following four things, the names of which begin with letter M. 1st Mohammedan, 2nd Mutrae or Step-mother, 3rd Mukhee or fly and 4th Mun or heart.

The Gooroo then ordered the Seikh woman to explain what was her belief, and she replied that she believes in serving the Gooroo and his Seikhs. O Gooroo you only are my protection, I will serve you with love, forgive me.

Then the Seikh woman and her husband served the Gooroo and giving presents, bent their heads before him.

---

[1] Name of 8th Sakhee.

[2] In Goormookhee, this phrase consists of 8 letters only thus, वा गु रु जी स हा य (1 2 3 4 5 6 7 8)

The Gooroo was pleased and praying for her, said you shall now have a son, and in your seventh birth, you shall become the wife of my Seikh " Sungat Singh" and will then obtain salvation. Here ends the 9th Sakhee.

SAKHEE TENTH.

Once in the presence of the Gooroo some skillful songsters and musicians sung the comedy of Gopee Chund, the Gooroo, and the assembly of his attendant Siekhs were pleased to hear it. It was morning time. The harmony of tone and the sweet sound of musical instruments mingled with the deep interest expressed by the singers were excellent. In that party there was a songster of Seikh religion, who loved to sing nothing but Gooroo's verses. He came to the Gooroo next morning and complained saying O Gooroo, your songsters have become faithless for they gave up your verses and began to sing " Gopee Chund's " story in the morning. Without Gooroo's verses other songs are imperfect, why did those Seikhs then begin to sing other stories than Gooroo's words ? The Gooroo replied, O simple brother, there is no difference between a Seikh and Gooroo, for, Seikhs, religious men, and lovers of God, do all remember the name of God at every breath, being disdainful towards the world. Seikhism is very far. O my Seikh ! well-deserving of praise is the King Gopee Chund, who left his 1400 wives, and the whole of his kingdom like a leaf of grass and retired from the world and applying himself strictly to devotion became a complete Sage. He resorted to the protection of Gooroo Gorukh Nath and obtained salvation. You all, though present before me, have your minds fixed in your " one-eyed", ugly, and dirty wives, and are always thinking that if something be obtained from the Gooroo, you may take it for those wives. How can you become like Gopee Chund ? The Gooroo is common to all, whose feelings are devoted to religion. Whatever words impart, tranquillity, desire to leave the world and the true knowledge, are equal to Gooroo's words. Useless verses, even of the Veda should be rejected and the words of gods, if they be useless, should be given up. Any thing said by a child, if it contains the essence of truth, should be accepted. Here ends the 10th Sakhee.

SAKHEE ELEVENTH.

Once, when the Gooroo was sitting in Durbar, a Seikh, who loved the ways of Gooroo complained against the Gooroo's sonsgters and said, that in a morning he was reading the sacred treaties of Sukhmunee and had only last section to finish, when the sonsgters began to sing, he told them to stop till he had finished it, they did not hear him notwithstanding he warned them that he will have them fined by the Gooroo : "Now do justice in my case O true king", the Seikh exlaimed. The Gooroo replied, whoever begins to talk when God's praises are to be sung is greatly liable to fine. O brother Seikh, you were feeding Seikhs with parched grain, and they began to feed them with bread. The Gooroo is pleased with them, for in the Kaliyug the only true protection is the name of God. O brother! whoever will sing or read the Gooroo's words through love, shall be saved from world and shall be a friend of the Gooroo, by whose favor all the Sungat,[1] if faithful, obtains salvation. The Veda's saying is that a man resorting to Gooroo's protection obtains rich enjoyments in this world, and salvation in that is to come. Here ends the 11th Sakhee.

SAKHEE TWELVTH.

One day a Seikh while reading "Oonkar-Banee"[2]

[1] An assembly of Seikhs.

[2] A chapter of Punch-Grunthee, which is a much respected book of Seikh religion.

repeated the following verse:—"Kurte kee mut Kurta jane *ke* jane Gooroo Soora," which means, "the Creator's ways are only known to the Creator; what does the brave Gooroo know!" The Gooroo hearing this verse repeated by the Seikh, ordered the reader to be beaten with a stick and to be brought before him. It was done so. The Gooroo made him sit afar. Other Seikhs begged, O true king why have you punished this Seikh? The Gooroo replied, that Seikh did not read my word with correctness. The Gooroo then called the punished Seikh near him and ordered him to repeat the verse. He read it as before. The Gooroo then ordered him to read this way, "Kurte kee mut Kurta jane *kai* jane Gooroo Soora," which means, "Creator's ways are known either to the Creator Himself or to the brave Gooroo. The Gooroo then commented that God's ways are only to God or to the Gooroo, if he is a holy and intelligent man. Other people hear these from the Gooroo and know. Had this not been the case, it should have been dark all over. The Gooroo then continued to say that the fault for which the Seikh was punished, is that he read the word के (ke) instead of कै (kai), which reduced the meaning of the verse to utter nonsense. If the first meaning be true, then why one should go to Gooroo's protection, which, therefore, becomes useless? O Seikh brother! one who ever will read my word correctly, will be happy. If it be wrong, he should repeat it with correctness. A man amends the spoiled thing of his house, why should he not then read Gooroo's word exactly? Such persons are said to be void of spiritual love. The Gooroo then repeated this verse of "Akal Oosut,[1]" "Bhawna Baheen Jug Jare-ee Marat hain," which means, "People without faith and sacred love die and perish in doubts." O Seikh there are 5 sorts of Seikhism, viz.,

---

[1] Literally God's praise.

1 Dhunde ke.

2 Dekha Dekhee.

3 Hirsee.

4 Sidkee.

5 Bhaw ke.

1. The first are those, who assume Seikhism for the sake of mingling in the society and to be saved from the censure of being called "Be-goora," or without spiritual guide.

2. Those who assume Seikhism for the sake of wealth, that is seeing that other men have risen to greatness by becoming a Seikh. Such persons are only fond of money and do not love Gooroo.

3. Those, who assume Seikhism by imitation, that is seeing a large crowd following that way and not learning about themselves, and the customs and manners of Seikhism and not knowing the mysteries of the Gooroo "Pahool."

4. Those, who assume Seikhism through faith.

5. Those, who assume Seikhism through the sacred love, Baba Nanuk's saying is, "Whoever has sought and found the true and complete Gooroo, can obtain his desires. Repeat the Name of God every day, O brother, and remember Him in breathing and eating." Here ends the 12th Sakhee.

SAKHEE THIRTEENTH.

After this the Sungat asked O Gooroo, what is the sacred origin of "Pahool?" What are the advantages of it? The Gooroo replied and said O brother there are 3 sciences by which supernatural powers are exercised, viz.,

1 Munter, 2 Junter, 3 Tunter. So our Munter is the "Sut Nam" or "True Name." Our Junter the letters of "Wah Gooroo" and our Tunter is water, sugar and iron. Water is given by Burmah God, Sugar by Inder God and iron by Yama. By means of these, mind is greatly put to rest, desire of worldly enjoyments is quenched by sugar and the sight of arms encourages the heart and creates a desire of becoming a hero of the field. "Churn Pahool," which was formerly in use, imparted faith and desire of serving Gooroo, but now as I was anxious to take field against Mahammedans, I appointed this Pahool of sword and ordered the wearing of Kes and the fixing of mind on Devi goddess and the reading of ten "Nirban" "Sawayas" with love and emotion, and the reading of Anund Sahib, and that of a section of "Jupjee" for salvation. By this Pahool a person will obtain "Dhurm" or religion, "Dhun" or wealth, "Kam" or desired objects, "Mokh" or salvation. A man wearing Kes without the Pahool ceremony is like a woman. The Gooroo then continued to say that his mother "Goojree" had asked a similar question and the same reply was given to her. The Seikh further asked O Gooroo, should we believe in God's power or Devi's power. The Gooroo replied that it is not proper to explain the mysteries of God, and kindness flows from mere pleasure. However, when a pupil of a true faith asks, it becomes necessary for the Gooroo to explain it. O brother, Unity is the principal of Gooroo's religion. Man should not entertain idea of difference even by inadvertence. I had in some previous age devoted myself to prayer and adorations in a forest of "Bindhachul" mountain. In the same forest and at the same time, "Ooma" had also been engaged in devotions, when at the request of Burmah, Devtas had taken her to heavens. The power of demons had in those days prevailed throughout the world. The Uuma or Brahmanee fought with the demons for many years and tried to kill "Rukt Beej" by whose

blood so many demons flourished as its drops fell on the ground. These demons increased to such a great number as would be represented by the figure of one (1) with hundred dots after it. All these were killed by Devi. The blood flowed like the waters of the great flood on the earth. The world became vacant and was hidden like stones in a river. Devi's army fled, some with and some without fighting. Devi then vanished and made herself an image of stone at "Bindhachul" mountain. The demons were also reduced to much difficulty and pain. Two of these demons named Sobel and Bel went to the above-mentioned devotee and exclaimed, Ah! Ah! who has taken away the woman. The devotee said, do not prate foolishly. God's power is always complete. Hearing this the wanton, stubborn and stupid demons ran to beat the "Samoond" devotee with the shouts of kill! kill! The devotee thought that it was neither his nor his pupil's business to fight, they being Brahmans devoted to God. The devotee had a floor of lion's skin under him, which he pushed a little with his hand and uttered the sound Hoon! By the effect of this a glorious person sprung out and fought with the demons for 10,05,000 years. The Devi was then enraged and came out of the image and after destroying all the demons spoke to the person, who had sprung from the lion skin spread under the devotee and said, you have assisted me in the fighting, in lieu of which I promise that I will appear to you whenever you will call for my assistance. I am pleased, ask whatever you desire from me. You will be henceforth called "Doosht Duman." I make all the persons now existing, your followers. You should fix your attention on my image. The devotee asked that I may be called by the name of "Singh" and be allowed to wear long hairs, and may be allowed to keep my loins without thread and the glory of arms, poetical genius, success of words, worldly enjoyments and salvation be granted to me. In addition to this I may get an opportunity of fighting with the enemies of Devtas. Devi hearing this, spoke that in the first part of 4th Yog, Rooder will appear in the world and will be called by the name of "Shunker." Vishnoo will come down and appear as his sister's son. I will also at that time being called by you, will appear to you. You should adopt my dress, i. e. red cloth dress, should not beautify your eyes with the antimony and should not enslave yourself to the love of your family. Saying this, the goddess began to lick the person and becoming extremely pleased with him gave a knife, a wrist-ring and Pranda[1] and said as you have sprung up from the "Khul" or lion-skin of the devotee, your name will be called "Khalsa" and your glory will at first be as great as that of a lion, but will be followed by decrease as the effect of intoxicating drugs. Your body will undergo troubles. Saying this the goddess went away and that person went to his father, the devotee, who told him, O my son I will be your father in that world also, but will not see you fighting in your boyhood. You have saved me and obtained Devis' favors, go on the bank of Godaveree river and apply yourself to hard devotions. As you have sprung up like a plant of "Gobhee" (cabbage) I give you the name of Gobind and the degree of "Singh" (lion) has already been given to you by the Devi. Hearing this and paying respects to the devotee by falling prostrate before him, the person went away and going on the bank of river, engaged himself in the devotions, and while immersed in contemplation, lo! it so happened that his spirit imperceptibly escaped from that body and was born as Gooroo Gobind Singh from the womb of "Bhagun" the wife of Tegh Bahadur, who was the incarnation of that devotee. Gooroo Gobind Singh was yet a child when both his father and mother left their worldly bodies and went

---

[1] A thing made of long silken threads, which Indian women tie at the end of their interwoven hairs.

to heaven. I am that person, the destroyer of the wicked, called here by the name of Gobind Singh. I possess all the qualities of a devotee, and all my Sungat is Khalsa and the power I possess is the fruit of Devi's favors and my hard devotions.

Bhai Boodha then said, write down, O writer! I relate to you what I have heard. The story of the great Gooroo is such that its mysteries cannot be perceived. The Gooroo, then, finishing this account, went upstairs of his house, I followed him, the Gooroo was pleased and told me, O Boodha, May you live long! *Your* house is beyond, and *ours* on this side of the river. This phrase the Gooroo repeated three times and looked at me and granted me a shield, a dagger, and a knife. Here ends the 13th Sakhee.

SAKHEE FOURTEENTH.

Once the Gooroo was sitting on the banks of a river and was attended by other Seikhs. He was silent and one Chouree-walla[1] named Soonak Singh was very near. The Gooroo began to pelt the Sungat with stones and to read the verse, which means, "The old men, women and the young persons are pressed by young demons, they could neither sleep nor wake nor cry out, to complain." All the Sungat fled, but Choureedar remained fearless. Nine hours after this, the Gooroo recovered his senses and was addressed by the "Surbundee"[2] Soonak Singh, who said tell me O Gooroo, how is to happen in the future. A man should offer his body, mind, and wealth to the true Gooroo, so I have found such a Gooroo, but we are cultivators of Bunjára Gôt, explain to us the meaning of the verse. The Gooroo replied O brother, Sungat has

---

[1] A servant whose duty it is to wave a fly-brush over his master's head.

[2] A native of Surbund between Loodiana and Umballa.

become faithless, therefore such faithless will die and shall be born again in the house of Seikhs and will suffer; then they will know that the Gooroo had told them the truth. O Bhai at the time of Devi's war the demons fled to their spiritual guide, Bhargav Moundee, who said, do not fear I will secure you the kingdom through my devotions. He passed the whole of Dawaper Yuga in devotions, at the end of which demons reflourished under the name of Toorj[1] and began to give rich feasts and to perform hard devotional exercises. The Devtas were deprived of their virtues and being accompanied by Brahma, complained before Vishnu, and cried out, Save us and make the demons give up their good actions, Vishnu treated the Devtas with respect and permitted them to go. Afterwards Vishnu descended on earth and was known as incarnation of Budh. In this body he made impure appearance, separate from Devtas, and dispraised the doctrines of Veda and the ceremonies of the world. By sweet and charming words reduced the Toorj to his subjection, and this made them leave their good actions. The Toorj were thus weakened and the Devtas began to beat them. Their Gooroo Bhargav, fled and betook himself to the country of women who were panting for a man. There were two queens in that country, whom the refugee enjoyed and made pregnant. He then wanted to depart from that country, when the two queens told him, "how will these children be nourished? Give them some name and show them your own country. The refugee said one born from Ees woman shall be called "Eesa" and the other born of Moos woman shall be called "Moosa." I give them every kind of power. I belong to Munoo country, where the descendants of these children will go and enjoy the life of a man. They will come "Phirke" that is by round way, and shall hence be called "Phirungee" or Englishmen and Phurasees or French. Here ends the 14th Sakhee.

[1] i. e. Toorks or Mahammedans.

SAKHEE FIFTEENTH.

Before 5000 years of the Kuliyuga will pass *i. e.* before 1899 A. D., the following things will happen. This account is given correctly. I explain to my Seikh according to Vedas. My followers may not disperse. O Ardasia hear the nice word! We will conquer Patul Nager in the morning. The rulers of Seikhs and Englishmen will join. My weak Seikhs will become powerful and my powerful Seikhs will become weak. Some things are foretold by Astrology, those you should also consider to be according to my belief. I have given to my Khalsa full glory for as long as they obey my following orders :—

1*st*. They should not be entangled in the love of wife and son.

2*nd*. They should not drive out their daughters like a herd of cows.

3*rd*. They should not sell their daughters in marriage and again pretend to be so respectable as to sit on carpets to distribute justice.

4*th*. They shoud not read Veda's words and give up the Gooroo.

5*th*. They should not follow Brahman's religion, and live as head-shaved devotees.

6*th*. They should not bring Mahammedan women in their houses.

7*th*. They should not be such as enslaved to prostitute for ever.

8*th*. They should not seek for Peers and leave the Gooroo far distant.

The woman shall do full justice, hear, O Seikh of Gooroo! the force of Seikhs and martyrs will remain till 1000 years. All the Seikh women will love their servants

The wives of Princes will become disobedient and unfaithful to their husbands. Fifty-nine years of the age of Ganges will remain to pass at that time. I will show displeasure till eight years, after which one of my martyr Seikhs will be born on earth and will reign over the kings up to Calcutta. The light of his glory will spread in the world and assuming the appearance of a Singh and being accompanied with his army he, the Daleep Singh will drive his elephant through the world. The Englishmen will first reign in Loodiana and will press his glory. Anxiety will prevail on the minds of all kings. All will pray for death. The beautiful women will fly to obtain wealth. The Khalsa will be much in distress at that time. The lamp (*i. e.* Daleep Singh) will shine in Khalsa. Daleep Singh will be the Emperor over all the kings. I will first explain to you the Bhimishut[1] Purb as detailed by Bias Rikh. A Brahmachari[2] of previous birth assumed the body of Akbar and well discharged his duties towards God, An Englishman had made himself servant of "Shahjahan," the son of Jahángeer. His power increased day by day and all the people felt it in their mind. At that time "Aurungzeb," who falsely pretended to be a retired man, began to serve Meeran Shah with a view of raising himself by that means. He left this service afterwards and killed his brother. He did not resign throne, but cutting off the head of Dara Shukoh his brother damaged the empire. Aurungzeb then began to reign and became our enemy without cause. He will use his force to wound the Khalsa in heart and killing Hindoos would like to spread the Mahammedan religion. He used to fly to Mukka on every Friday and there prayed for being chosen by God. One night, a voice was heard that a powerful man will rise over all. In the morning the dream became true. He saw Mahammedans far reduced and Hindoos

---

[1] Book of Prophecies in Hindoo religion.

[2] A retired Brahman.

increased to millions. He then ordered that he will make all of one religion, having proclaimed his order he wanted us to show him the miracles and on that pretence began enmities with us and did not consider what was ordained by God. He will make friendship with all the Rajahs and will draw his forces against us. By Gooroo's favor we will kill all, who have embraced Mahammedanism in battle. The Mahammedans will live without glory and will earn their bread by labor and will no longer be rulers. I will leave my body at the age of 43 years. After that all the Seikhs will leave their bodies by and by and will come Kings and Chiefs in the next brith. The Seikhs will die while engaged in killing, and plundering. There shall be no end of the number of heads cut off. One Bheen Singh will conquer the city, the villages and the streets will be plundered. I will also put on a body about 40 years after the Hindoo Sal 1800. The Mahammedans of Kandhar will come and return and will desolate the country with all the villages. In the 19th year, after this, a King named "Rung Tees" will flourish in city. This King will come from the east, beating and killing as he comes. The foot-army of Jesus Christ will come. Khalsa will be divided. There will be quarrels and dissentions between men and women in all families. They will leave the arms and will become like Brahmins. Such things will remain till 33 years. My Seikhs will flourish 7 years earlier. The women will die in a way opposite to the virtue. No one of the Seikh rulers will be allowed to remain. If in that time a Seikh trader will arise and will go about in astonishment in the search of religion. Dissentions will arise in Calcutta, there will be quarrels and distress in each house. Nothing will be known for 12 years. Daleep Singh, the Master, will be born. I will then assist him secretly and will fight for 21 years. The Englishmen will also come to the Seikhism and making friendship with the people will establish themselves. A Mahammedan named

Bundan will arise, who will distress the people and destroy their castes. He will be tyrant for the world as lion for a cow. His reign will exist for 1000 years. There is no doubt in this. In the village "Rilpoor"* there will flourish a carpenter's son, who will reign by force. In the Punjab country there had born a man of Sood caste, who had been this path of death. There will be a King of Delhie, reigning over the east, north and south of India. He shall be a man possessed of supernatural power. Something has been revealed, but much remains unrevealed. The story of the creator is very extensive.

When the Mahammedans will distress the people of Kashmeer, a son will be born in the house of Bishen Dutt Brahman. He will be an incarnation of Deity and shall be called "Kulgee Awtar." He will establish good customs in the world. He will be born in the "Sunbhul" village. At that time 10,000 years of the Kuliyuga will pass away. He will thus be a Seikh of the Gooroo, in whom he shall believe and to whom he will make offerings of Karah Prashad. He will not eat Sheernee. When he will become 12 years old, he will marry a woman named "Trikota." He will kill Maleches or Mahammedans and will establish a strong religion. He will live for 55 years in the world. When they would like to snatch the wife of that Brahman, then he will show power. He will be like Parasram, who lived in "Tretayuga." He will possess Brahma-glory, by the effect of which he will execute all his works. After this, the result of the devotions of Vishnu Shurma[1] will come to light. I have related the story before you in detail, O my Seikh! I will also be born in the house of a Brahman. Till that time my Sungat will be engaged in the service of Baital and assembly of Shaheeds or martyrs. They will take offerings

* The Cookas call this Rilpore by the name of Ryavándi and this carpenter's son is said to be one Ram Sing the leader of the Cookas.

[1] *i. e.* Vishnoo Dutt Brahman above said.

from the brother of "Ravan" and will not take notice of Brahmans and Seikhs. I have revealed this secret about the future, whoever will read or hear it, will come to me. Sakhee 15th finished.

SAKHEE SIXTEENTH.

Once the Gooroo had dressed himself in white clothes and was sitting near a wall, which was being plastered by a seikh; a drop of mud fell upon the Gooroo's clothes. The Gooroo then ordered his Sungat to give the plastering seikh a slap. Hearing this all the Sungat ran and began to beat the seikh with slaps. Gooroo felt that the fault has been light but the punishment heavy. Thinking this he said, the Sungat of the Gooroo is, of course, obedient, but O my seikhs this man was also a seikh of the Gooroo and you have given him a slap of his "Kases," this you have done bad. Kases are a sign of Seikhism, whosoever will commit fault against these, will be an enemy of the Gooroo. You have committed a great sin. If you make an excuse that you have done this by the Gooroo's order, the answer is that Gooroo has only passed order for one slap and not for many. This Seikh is your religious brother, therefore, as an atonement of your fault against him, you should better give him your daughter in marriage. Hearing this all the Sungat remained silent. The Gooroo then said a true Seikh is that who obeys all the orders of the Gooroo. Seikhism is very far, O brothers you are all nominal Seikhs. In the meantime a Kundharee seikh brought his daughter and made her stand before the Gooroo, who blessed her and said, be happy! O seikh, you have shown your true, faith to the Gooroo, who has guarded your Seikhism. The plastering seikh spoke out that this girl is to me like sister. I will not marry her. The girl spoke out "that my father has given me away by the Gooroo's order, I will now remain in the presence of the Gooroo." The Gooroo then said Kanaits[1] were born from a girl. In the territory of Raja Bulubh Chund people used to sell their daughters for they were reduced to poverty. "Nund Raj" notwithstanding of his being called a Maharaja had extracted all the money from his subjects and had buried it in the ground. The number of his subjects was therefore greatly reduced. Rajah Bulubh ordered his men to take girls from the subjects in lieu of tax. According to this order all the Rajah's servants jumped and fell over the girls, who all conceived. Those who were born from these girls were called *Kanaits.* The Rajah then gave these daughters in marriage to all his servants in certain cases granting three girls to one man and in some cases one to two. The old custom was broken and a new one observed. What does it matter, continued the Gooroo, O Bhai Kahn Singh, you also accept the daughter of this Seikh in marriage. From the womb of this girl you shall have five sons. He (the Seikh of Malwa country) then married this girl by "Anund ceremony" and took her to his house, five villages were peopled by the descendants of the issues of this marriage.

Bhai Boodha, then, said, this Sakhee was recited to me by Soojan Singh Lahouree, I have not seen this with my own eyes. His son Baisakha Singh still knows it. Here ends the 16th Sakhee.

SAKHEE SEVENTEENTH.

Once Gooroo Gobind Singh's mother said, to him, O my son, I am a light minded woman and my heart fails on account of love I have towards you, as I have not

---

[1] A family of Rajpots.

seen your face since a long time. Your father also departed early to the next world. I have to-day come alone to you. O my son! ! you are Gooroo of Gooroos and my powerful son. See in what condition I am ! Neither you speak with me nor does the intensity of my love towards you leave me alone. Our fellow kinsmen say that you had applied yourself to hard devotions in order to make the Devi appear before you, hence you became deaf and dumb. Some say you failed in that, as the Brahman, who directed you in your worship fled away from you, as he felt afraid from "Kuliyug." Now explain to me these things. The Gooroo thinking that Father and Mother are the real Gooroos took her aside and made her sit on a flat piece of stone and addressed her saying it is not good to reveal the secrets of a Devta, but as you insist, I am obliged to say. When I left "Pawla" village, it came to my mind, to what god I should worship, in order that my religion be reverenced in the world. For this purpose I searched all the places. I then called Kesho Dass Brahman, who was a resident of Kanshee and was like a lamp in all the "Sarsoot" Brahmans of that age. He was in constant habit of worshipping the sun and always repeated his (sun's) Munter. Then I went to battle in "Kapal Mochun Tank" and was thinking day and night as long as I lived there. The army of Mahammedans searching after me arrived. God is the protection of all. When I betook to a jungle near Narainpoor and lost my senses being fully absorbed in the sacred love of God. I then went to live in a small garden of mangoe trees, situated near Munee Majra[1] under which a fine canal flowed day and night. In that place Muthra Misser met me like Seikhs and looked at me as a Gooroo. He was a good poet and knowing me as a Gooroo, he paid reverence to me. I put[2] my hand on his head, and told him that he was like

[1] A town in the district of Loodiana.

[2] Signs by which devotees bless.

Krishna to the followers of Gooroo Nanuk. I then departed from Munee Majra and crossing "Dhunki" field passed by a village of Brahmans. There lived a girl, who made compliments to me. Seeing her faith I went to live in her house. I had a Koomait horse with me, to which the girl served very much. In lieu of this I granted salvation to her. I had Mohur Singh and the following Seikhs are in my attendance in those days, *viz.*, Nund Singh and Sahib Zemindars, Boodh Singh Barbour, Sudda Singh Bhut,[1] Muthra Brahman, Lohta Jheewur, Mulwa the cooker, the son of Mumoo. Seven days after that I thought it in my mind that I should worship and please Naina Devi and thus obtain her assistance in destroying Mahammedans. I was induced to execute this plan by Dhunna Brahman. I gave leave to all my attendants to depart and myself accompanied with the Brahman went up the hill and entered in a small cave. It was Thursday and 11th of the lunar month, and the moon was in "*Pookh* Nahsatter," at that time. I determined to perform the strict ceremonial worship of Devi and began to Human of 5 Pahirs or 15 hours, appointing other persons to discharge the several different duties. On the following day I commenced 12 Pahirs Human[2] and put Devi's image before me, I then became motionless like a wall and repeated, "Oon[3] Oon, Moon Moon, Goon Goon, Roon Roon," spell of 16 letters. Kishen Misser wanted some reward the from me. I told him that he being a Sarsoot swatt Brahman was like a father to me and I was to him like a son. He became extremely pleased and told me that he was only trying me and that he considered me as a part of his body. That he knew I was like earth in forbearance, and that I was a blessed person, in determin-

[1] A bard.

[2] A special form of sacrifice among the Hindoos, by which, sugar, purified butter and ingredients are put in the fire, verses of the praises of Devi being repeated at the same time.

[3] These letters if written in Goormookhee would consist of 16 letters only.

ing to perform the important sacrifice by which salvation may be obtained for the whole of my family. He then told me be cautious to apply myself closely to Jup,[1] to be silent, and to keep the body clear and pure. Hearing this the Gooroo's mother became more anxious and the Gooroo's kindness increased. The Gooroo then continued to say, O mother, I gave up my house and rest, and began to eat very little. I then commenced Huma of Ghee and Til[2] and did not move my eye-lids till 5 months. I then saw Devi in a dream speaking to me and saying that. she cannot appear in shape of Devtas in this age of Kuli-yuga, but I will appear to you in the shape of a glorious woman. Nine months after this, on the 9th day of lunar month at 3 o'clock in the evening the above said dream was verified. Kishen Misser had informed me previously that Devi would appear to me shortly and would ask for offerings of human body. That I should serve her well. The Brahman then told me that he saw this dream while waking. He then went to procure offerings and directed me to be cautious and to apply myself closely in the sacred contemplations of Kali, who shall appear now or in the following morning and that I should not fear at that time and keep my mind strong. In the absence of Kishiva Misser my heart failed a little. According to the Misser's predictions at 2 o'clock in the afternoon a great light appeared in hills. So strong and powerful was this light, that in comparison to this, lightning, moon and sun were nothing. A lustre descended from heavens and came towards the earth. My eyes were closed and I stood with fear. The shape of a woman glanced before my eyes and asked me what do you want? Your worship has been complete. Hearing this I was absorbed in extreme pleasure and lost my senses, Devi laughed and said O my son

---

[1] The repetition of incantatious, the account of which is remembered with a string or beads.

[2] The seed of Sesamun.

where are my offerings. Then said lo! I have granted you the religion of Kases.[1] I then praised Devi, who was pleased and promised to appear to me whenever I call for her assistance. Devi then spoke to me as follows "shut your eyes I am going." I reveal to you how your religion will flourish. The Mahammedans will rule over India till the Hindee year 1840, after which they will be destroyed, your desire will be fulfilled. Believe what I say to be true. Take this my knife understand this to be my body, and stir up the sugar-mixed-water with it at the Pauhul occasions. Wear this knife on head. Whoever will take Pauhul by this ceremony will be called a hero in the battle, Saying this Devi wanted me to offer her something. I pierced my body with a knife and gave her a drop of blood. Then Lunkra[2] then asked something from me and said he only wants two things, *i. e.* a Kuchh[3] and something to eat, and if I give him these, he will assist me in battle and will not let the honor of Seikhism fall. Having said this and taken their presents Devi's attendants went away. I felt a desire of leaving all wordly concerns. The Gooroo then prohibited his mother from asking him further about the Devis' sayings. The mother was pleased to hear so much and went away. The Gooroo then distributed all his property to the poor. The Boodha then said to Sahib Singh O brother Gooroo's works cannot be understood for the people of his family and village, began to say that he leaving all his property become mad. The enmity was created with all the hill Rajahs, who began to confuse the Gooroo's power. All the Seikhs came to assist the Gooroo. In the morning of a certain day, Kishis Misser came to the Gooroo, who with folded hands told him, O Misser by your kindness and through the effects of your spells Devi

---

1

2 A body-guard of Devi.

3 Breeches reaching to the knees.

was pleased with me and granted me the respected position of a Gooroo, I will give you $1\frac{1}{4}$ lakhs of rupees. Having said this the Gooroo embraced him and said O Misser where I am *there* you shall be and *i. e.* shall live together. All the persons of science and art will respect you. Hearing this Keshive wept and said, O Sir, I desired the same what you have said. The Gooroo could not give to the Brahman what he had promised to hence the Brahman went away.

One day a person named Hookum Singh of the Sodhee family and one of the constant attendents of the Gooroo asked, O Gooroo to what place has *Misser* fled. The Gooroo replied "O Brother he has died and born in another body. He shall be my Seikh in that birth and will be called by the name of Ram Singh. He will be a king and will fight with many and will reign for a long time. In his 3rd birth he will be born in Lahore and after his death will "join me." Here ends the 17th Sakhee.

SAKHEE EIGHTEENTH.

Once a body of Seikhs complained before the Gooroo against the Cooker, saying, that he puts forward objections in distributing food. The Gooroo laughing replied, the Cooker he has enjoyed the free wealth of the Gooroo and has consequently become covetous. He is a "Musnud" and a fellow very hungry of last birth, lo! The sword will belong to the Gooroo and the Deg[1] will belong to the Wah-Gooroo there will be much taste in the Deg. One who will not eat food given out of the Deg will not be a true Seikh. O Seikh brothers prepare the food yourself with purity. Whosover will distribute food will be

---

[1] Persons who were appointed by Nanuk's followers to collect presents for the Gooroo from among his Seikhs, who were scattered over in distant countries. These persons by obtaining rich presents and able to embezzle them had grown extremely wicked.

blessed. Gooroo's religion is separate from all religions. First you should read "Ardass"[1] and then distribute the food and then repeating the words "Tav Prashad"[2] you should begin to eat it. In the end you should read Choli,[3] you should always take care of horses and arms, you should be at enmity with Mahammedans and separate from and should not make friendship with hill-men. The Gooroo will provide for your expenses. The Khutrees and Saniasees will be subject to the voice of Khalsa. Whoever will hide away a part of food served before him, or will ask for more after he has been satisfied or will look with a lustful eye towards the family-women of another Seikh, will be made to suffer the pains of millions of hells and will not be mine. No one should condemn the food served before him and whosever will give hungry to eat will earn the goodness fruits of a Yog. Here ends the 18th Sakhee.

SAKHEE NINETEENTH.

Once the Gooroo was told by his relatives and Seikhs to give up all hostile feelings towards the Hill-Rajahs and to be friendly with them as they wished to compromise with the Gooroo. The Gooroo replied we cannot trust in these mean fellows, let us try then and let Gooroo's treasure be sent to Malwa. The Gooroo's camp was all armed besieged by Hill-men, who had sworn that they will not be, any more, hostile to the Gooroo. Having seen 5000 bullocks laden with treasure, were moved by ambition and began to plunder them. When they touched the loads they found nothing but stones, bricks and earth filled in the hemp bags. The Gooroo had previously de-

---

[1] Some verses in which the sacred names of Devi and ten Gooroos are repeated, generally read by Seikhs in the beginning of important commencements.

[2] This food is granted by you O'God.

[3] Verses in thanksgiving to god for giving such a food.

vised this plan in order to try the faith of Hill-men, for he knew all the secrets. The Hill-men were irritated. The Góoroo said, we should not trust enemies. Khalsa will revenge these hostilities. These Hill-men will not enjoy peace. O Seikhs fraud is very bad, it is better to kill a man than to treat him fraudulently. The Gooroo's relations also henceforth began to put their faith in him. And believed his words to be true, but were not fully contented. Here ends the 19th Sakhee.

SAKHEE TWENTIETH.

Once Toorks,[1] as requested by the Hill-Rajas, came to fight with Gooroo. A heavy battle ensued. One, Saida Beg Moghul an Officer of Toorks, deserted them and joining with the followers of the Gooroo fought against them and having conquered them presented himself before the Gooroo, who exclaimed! "Be of long age! well have you fulfilled your promise"! you are Kundhree, the Gooroo continued, "and will therefore understand better what I meant by these words. You had in previous births met with Baba Nanuk, whom you had served in the garden. I had told you at that time that I will call you and see your arms. You had been moved at that time to hear the effective holy songs of Baba Nanuk and had addressed him saying, you possess full power of miracles, who is it, even out of jins (spirits) that does not obey you." Hearing this the Moghul[2] fell upon the Gooroo's feet and said all this was true, O Gooroo, save me now. He then gave up his camps and property to be plundered and began to live in the presence of the Gooroo, who granted him arms. He killed Raja Hurree Chand with a sword while fencing with him. The both of them were well-skilled in the art of fencing, but Gooroo had secretly

---

[1] Army of Mahammedan's emperor.

[2] *i. e.* Saidage,

and miraculously assisted him, the Mogul. He again fenced with Dena Begh, who was friend of Hill-Rajahs, but was, this time, killed by a sword and his soul went to heavens by Gooroo's favor. This was a wonderful prodigy which happened. Here ends the 20th Sakhee.

SAKHEE TWENTY-FIRST.

Once the Gooroo defeated Hill-Rajahs, who fought vigorously. The army of all the Rajahs, were, Hundooree, Kulooree, Chundel, Wuzeer Singh Futtahpoorea, Shive Surn Nahneea, amounted to 10,000 men, when Khalsa amounted to only 800. The Hill soldiers were killed and destroyed by the following arms, *viz*, Swords, Tegho,[1] spears, guns, javelins, shields and Bows. The voice Douroo[2] drum prevailed in the battle. The heroes were roaring in the field and the heads were being cut off. The sword played every where and ill-behaved princes were being slain. The Seikhs gained the victory and became fearless. The Gooroo was sitting at a distance and was inspecting the whole battle. A river of elephants and horses blood flowed. Happened what happened, the Khalsa was at last freed and Mountaineers defeated. The Gooroo, who was mounted on blue horse, saw the Khalsa and being filled with astonishment drew back. The Khalsa heard this and followed the Gooroo. The enemies pursued the Khalsa. The Seikh heroes made their horses run and were exclaiming loudly; one of them Nouruny Singh exclaimed. Stop, do not go further! O Blue horse,[3] I swear you by the name of Gooroo. The horse stood, notwithstanding the Gooroo stirred him and whipped him to move on. The Gooroo then dismounted and sat down and addressed the horse saying, O horse you were a Mu-

---

[1] A kind of sword, heavier and differently shaped from common swords.

[2] A kind of tambourine.

[3] The horse on which the Gooroo was mounted.

sund[1] in the last birth, and had been embezzling out of the offerings made to Gooroo by Seikhs. I know this with certainty. The horse, hearing this, trembled. The Gooroo then spoke out saying O Khalsa! I am yours and you are mine. Beat on! and destroy the armies. The Khalsa then returned and began to fight. The Gooroo, as he was sitting, discharged seven arrows, which caused cries to be raised in the hill-army. The Gooroo's army, overflowing with courage fell upon the enemy and returned victorious. The Gooroo was pleased and went on. It was all well. Here ends the 21st Sakhee.

SAKHEE TWENTY-SECOND.

Once a body of Songsters sang before the Gooroo excellently, and with emotions of sacred love, making the sound of the musical instrument called Dhoonk[2], the tone of their palate and the beating of time, all harmonious to each other. The Khalsa hearing this were pleased and exclaimed, well-done! well done! how nicely have these men sung! They have made us overflow with happiness! The Gooroo then uttered the following verse from his mouth, *viz.*, The Seikhs entreated the Gooroo to explainthis phrase to them. The Gooroo then recited the following story :—

There was a Lumberdar of a certain village, who was watering his field by means of a turning-well and had put his hoe on a bed of his field. Some one came and stole this hoe. The Lumberdar said to himself, if mine (who am chief of village) hoe is stolen, what will be the case with others. He called a drummer and caused it to be proclaimed by beat of drum. All the people heard it, but no one could procure the hoe for him. The Lumberdar be-

[1] Previously explained.
[2] A kind of stringed instrument of music rung by a large pin of wood.

gan to search in each house of the village, wondered at it, and some of them said it is better to search the house of drummer also. When it was done so, the hoe was found in a corner of the house. The Lumberdar then in the presence of all the people said to the drummer, O brother the hoe was in your house, why did you make all this noise abroad. You have not done well! The Lumberdar gave good advices to the drummer and dismissed him.

The Gooroo returned to his subject and said, hear! O Seikh brethren, these songsters are mere noise makers. Such is the case with all, Pundits[1] Padhas,[2] Astrologers, songsters, whoremongers, &c. &c. All these persons are apt to advise others, but do not feel contented in themselves. Hard devotions and divine worships by being performed do not impart glory. Man should follow the paths of virtue, notwithstanding it be troublesome, as he does not care to spend money in buying dear things. Those who continue in proceeding asking the right way from any one who met them at last reach at the desired height, but those who merely point out the way but do not move themselves, remain where they are; such presons who run to complete and understanding are very rare. O brothers whoever will understand the truth will swim across the ocean of the world. Whoever has found the true Gooroo, will be forgiven. Baba Nanuk says, "whoever succeeds in finding the true Gooroo, his account is cleared." Here ends the 22nd Sakhee.

SAKHEE TWENTY-THIRD.

Once there was a great famine in India, prices of grain had risen extremely and the people were filled with sorrow. The Gooroo seeing this began to distribute

[1] A learned Brahman.

[2] Brahman teacher.

grain. All the Rajahs wondered at this, and the Gooroo's mother, named Goojree, reduced the expenses of his kitchen. The seikhs informed the Gooroo that the mother had ordered them to reduce the kitchen expenses. That it is not known how long this scarcity will continue. The Gooroo became very angry to hear these words and exclaimed O "Oojnce,"[1] it is not proper to make reductions when the store is well provided. Such is the will of God! He continued to say, O brethren, the stewardship of women, Khutree,[2] mean fellows, new servants, minor girls, minor boys, and coward persons in general is very bad. O Seikh Brethren I know, that Mai [3] Goojree was instructed by her parents, my Musands, and the new servants. There are few Seikhs who are acquainted with the secrets of my heart. O Brother Kurm [4] was killed by Pandavs [5] in Mahabharuth war at the end of which Koontee, the mother of Pandavs said to his son Yodishter, the eldest of Pandavs to perform the funeral rites of Kurm, as he was also she said, one of her sons granted to her by the Sun while she was a virgin, and was, therefore, the eldest of all. Yudhister hearing this was enraged and said, O Sinner, why did you not inform me of this previously! that I should not have killed him and should have subjected myself to him as my eldest brother. Who will now be guiltly of killing him! Begone! and do not show me your face and henceforth I pray, that no women will be able to keep secrets in her mind, and the house where women will reign, shall be destroyed. The Gooroo further, said see, O brethren, by son's order Durgadhun[6] was killed and Raja Dushruth[7] dies

---

[1] Literally ruined. The name of the mother was Goojree, but the Gooroo being enraged called her by the name Oojree (leaving out G) which means ruined.

[2] A well-known caste of Hindoos.

[3] Means mother and the title by which old women are generally called.

[4] One of the famous heroes of Mahabharuth History. Here Gooroo refers to narrative of Mahabharuth in order to prove the foolishness of women.

[5] Five brothers heroes of Mahabharuth war.

[6] Famous character of Mahabharuth.

[7] The father of Rama, an incarnation of God according to Hindoos.

because he obeyed what Kaikai[1] said. The house, over which there are two persons to control, does not last, but is annihilated by calamities. My followers will kill, and plunder Khutrees. The Seikhs will pass the days of hardship in bushes of jungle. I will have skins of the Seikhs taken off from their body by the Mahammedans. The kings will be deprived of their kingdom. Cowards will become heroes and heroes will become cowards. The men will become slaves to the women. The women of seikhs I will make over to the descendants[2] of Christ. The religion of Christ will be discussed in each house. All this will happen within 40 years. I can extinguish the desires which my mother had hundred years ago. The Seikhs, then, intervened and caused the mother to be forgiven by the Gooroo, who becoming at last pleased, said that as long as the affair of my Lunger (cooking room) are well conducted, my curse will have no effect. But as soon as the lunger will stop, the curse will have full effect. The Gooroo turned away his face from the Seikhs and said. Let all the Seikhs go to Malwa, to see the Dumduma of the Gooroo which is a sacred place of Gooroo like the city of My Seikhs should serve Dumduma, and whosever does so will obtain the same blessings as one livingin Kanshee does. The house of the Gooroo is a place of salvation for the martyrs. Here ends the 23rd Sakhee.

SAKHEE TWENTY-FOURTH.

Once Seikhs asked the Gooroo O true king, what persons are called martyrs? The Gooroo laughed and said a mystery have you asked O Seikhs!! The Gooroo keeps his Sungat in his presence and protects the honor of his servants. The age of Kuliyoga so horrible, O Seikhs, Gooroo is a shepherd to reprove and to amend

---

[1] The younger wife of Dushruth.

[2] Meaning thereby followers of Christ, viz., Englishmen.

his Seikhs. Gooroo possesses the power of controlling Seikhs. Whosoever is strong in faith and brave in battle, he is saved, but one who is faithless and coward, will suffer the pains of innumerable births and deaths. The Gooroo accompanied by his attendants will wait for his Seikhs and assuming the body of 16 elements will protect his Seikhs till 10,000 years in order that the Seikhs may come to him. Every one who comes is included in the Khalsa assembly. Fifty-six Karors[1] of Seikhs have been made over to the Gooroo in the Kuliyoga. The order of God is that they may be purified and saved. The Gooroo waits for the Seikhs, and has an intercourse between the earth and heavens. The wishes of the Martyrs are always fulfilled and they rule over all the Bhoots,[2] Prets,[3] giants, men, animals, birds, nags,[4] yakhs,[5] Gundhurbs,[6] Apsarus,[7] &c. &c. The angels[8] of death go about with their permission. In the Shasters[9] they are called, Baitals and Biddiadhrs. Some of them are good and some bad. Their disposition are of 3 sorts, 1st Satkee (virtuous) 2nd Rajsee (moderately good) 3rd Tamsee (vicious). They cause themselves to be worshipped by their own (Sungat) followers, and grants them their wishes for enjoyments. They are givers of peace and trouble. The gods have made over "Bharuth khund" (the earth) to them, and have gone themselves to heavens. The things offered to the gods reach gods through them. The God has appointed them on this work. They are of many sorts. They have plenty of food, clothes, carriages, &c. &c. They

---

1 560,000,000.

2 A goblin.

3 Fiend.

4 In Hindoo Mythology, a race of serpents having human faces and inhabiting Patal or lower world.

5 A race of demigods inhabiting heavens.

6 Celestial musicians.

7 Female dancers in paradise.

8 In original "your doot."

9 Sanskrit Books of Hindoo religion.

They can walk in all Deeps[1] and Khunds[2]. They do not go astray about and see the fun of God's creation, as the ancient king Bepushchit had done. They do not become entangled in births and deaths. The Gooroo is standing over their head and guards them like a shepherd. This is the position of my Shaheeds (martyrs.) The Sungat of Naths are "Sidhs" and the followers of Mahammed are called "Jinat." Those who are followers of no Gooroo, become goblins and fiends. Here ends the 24th Sakhee.

SAKHEE TWENTY-FIFTH.

Once a beautiful and sweet-spoken boy came and paying homage to the Gooroo stood before him, at a distance. The Gooroo having seen him asked, O boy whose son you are? wherefrom are you coming? and what is your caste and family. The boy replied, O true king I am the son of Mumola, we are Gooroo's Seikhs, I am made Seikh by Khunda[3] Pauhool ceremony and my father was a Seikh of Churn[4] Pauhool ceremony. I am a resident of "Surhind" and am a goldsmith by caste. The Gooroo asked him O boy, the city of Surhind is populated or has become ruined? The goldsmith Seikh said, what the Gooroo's will is, so shall it be, but when I left it, it was populated. The Gooroo asked him whether any of his relations was with him. The boy replied his father had lately died and his mother was with him. The Gooroo said O boy you better live with your mother in my presence. The goldsmith hired the house of a Khutree

---

[1] A continent.

[2] A quarter, a religion, one of the nine sections of the world, as reckoned by the Hindoos.

[3] This ceremony was established by Gooroo Gobind Singh and means sword's Pauhool, as it was established for military purposes and the ceremony is performed by the sweet water being stirred with a sword or knife and then being given to drink and sprinkled over the head of the person who is to be made a Seikh.

[4] This ceremony was established by Baba Nanuk and is performed simply by drinking the water with which the feet of the Gooroo are washed.

and began to live with his mother in the Gooroo's presence. After many days the Gooroo asked him, O Seikh are you skilled in goldsmith's works. The boy said, yes Sir, by your favor I know it very well. The Gooroo ordered him to prepare an ornament worth 11 gold mohurs, which the treasurer was ordered to give to him. The boy prepared the ornament with great skill, and made it beautiful. The Gooroo was pleased to see it and ordered the treasurer to give whatever money the boy may want, and to get always ornaments prepared by him and to keep them in the treasury, as the Gooroo wants them. The Gooroo then asked the boy whether he was not habituated to any vice. The answered, no Sir, I have always lived in the good company of holy men. The Gooroo said where there is great virtue or skill, there is some vice attended with it. Baba Nanuk has said, "We should sacrifice ourselves to such a man, as will be virtuous, skilled and learned but unattended with vice." The goldsmith continued to prepare ornaments for the Gooroo and was treated with perfect confidence, no account being kept of his transactions. After a long time the Gooroo told to his treasurer to weigh secretly whatever gold to this time given to the goldsmith, whom he should not inform of this. After this twenty-four gold mohurs were given to the goldsmith for preparing bangles which when they were brought to the Gooroo and were weighed and found to be only 17 gold mohurs in weight. The Gooroo then ordered all the ornaments previously prepared to be weighed also. It was done so and all were found to be wanting. The Gooroo told him O boy you told us that you had always kept good company and had no vice! Now what is the meaning of vice? What you also possess some sort of virtue as Musnuds! Were you receiving no wages from the Gooroo. The boy felt ashamed. The Gooroo then said, the "Jut,[1] who uses the plough, is my true and

[1] Clown, cultivator.

dutiful Seikh." The Seikhs asked, O true king, people of all nations, such as Brahmans, Khutree, Lood and Bais, are thy Seikhs, why have you praised the Jut only? The Gooroo said, "Jut, Bhut,[1] Nut[2] and Dhunut[3] are faithful to their words and people of three castes are my true Seikhs, Jut, Bunjara[4] and all other Aroras[5]. The 3rd part of the Seikhism I have distributed to the rest of the world. But O brother others have adopted Seikhism merely for the sake of bread and obtaining their wishes. Baba Nanuk says, "What will be the use of Seikhism if there is no faith What will be the profit of trading if it is not carried on at large scale; what will the instructions of sacred Beds do, if the coveteousness is not relinquished; what be the advantage of high and respectable birth, if God's name is not remembered." O Nanuk blessed and fruitful are all the acts of the person, who knows the name of God! O brother, the Gooroo continued you should not trust the following all of which four thing have the betters in their beginning, *viz.*, (1) Soonar or goldsmith, (2) Sôukun or fellow-wife, (3) Supor serpent (4) Sher or lion. These four do not fail to do ill some time or the other. And the following four persons having letter K. in their beginning are always aspiring for pre-eminence, *viz.*, (1) Kazee or Mahammedan lawyer, (2) Kulal or wine seller, (3) Kanoongo, or superintendent of village-clerks, (4) Kusbee or prostitute. And the following four persons, whose names begin with the letter B, are extremely covetous, *viz.*, (1) Brahman,[6] (2) Bunyan,[7] (3) Bukhshee,[8] (4) Bunchun[9] or a thief. Saying this

---

1 Bards.
2 The name of a tribe who are jugglers, repedancers and tumblers.
3 Wealthy person.
4 Trader.
5 A low caste of Hindoos.
6 Priests of Hindoos.
7 Dealers in grain.
8 Paymaster of the army.
9 This is a Sanscrit word.

the Gooroo went to his place and the Seikhs came away to the respective dwellings. Here ends the 25th Sakhee.

SAKHEE TWENTY-SIXTH.

Once a Seikh complained before the Gooroo saying, "that Musunds went to my house and were served with Bread and Dâl, upon which they railed me and said, O wretch, cursed by the Gooroo, what! shall we eat Dâl[1] and bread? No, we want Karah[2] Prashad. I and my wife fell at their feet and said that we were very poor and could not provide for Karah[2] Prashad. They insisted and said Gooroo had ordered them always to eat Karah Prashad from Siekh's house. I was then obliged to mortage my wife's petticoat and to feed them with Karah Prashad and then gave them present for the Gooroo. O true king they thus put us to great inconvenience, what is your order! The Gooroo ordered that Musunds should be plundered and driven out, for the Gooroo said they bite the Siekhs like dogs. The Gooroo who causes trouble and inconvenience in this world, what protection he will give in the next! Hearing this, Seikhs plundered and imprisoned the Musunds for many days, after which the Gooroo caused them to be released and said, " My Seikhs should give only such presents as they can conveniently provide for, Musunds are not mine, I know them, they are as dreadful giants to the Seikhs. Hearing this Musunds bowed before the Gooroo and said O true king forgive us, in future we shall eat whatever Seikhs give us. Why are all punished for the fault of one person? The Gooroo said O Brother it is the age of "Kuliyoga" now, and the Seikhism depends upon faith. There is no want of money in the Gooroo's treasury. You should not now go to Seikh's house without being called. Musunds were thus

---

[1] Bisected corn boiled and salted generally eaten by Indians with the bread.

[2] A delicious expensive food, explained before.

stopped and as if it were began to die. They complained before the Gooroo's mother and said the income is stopped by the Gooroo! The mother came before the Gooroo and said O son, how shall affairs of the world be carried out! How shall the Lunger (cooking room) of the Seikhs be provided! Hearing this the Gooroo was filled with indignation and spoke out, O daughter of ruined family, you have concealed the Treasure of the 2 lakhs of Rupees and cannot provide for the Lunger of the Seikhs. The treasury is only for the Mahammedan enemies. Plunder and eat O Seikhs. the Gooroo ordered, I have seen the faith of the Seikhs, but my relatives are uncontented. Go, and eat wherever you find! The Seikhs then said, save us, O king. The Gooroo said O Brother, Baba Nanuk's saying is, that he will appear in the world in ten different dresses. So shall it be! The mother was silent and said, Oh for the good I had come, but a bad curse is obtained. Forgive O son I had came to you knowing that you were my son. The Gooroo said, O mother, go and obtain the good will of Khalsa, who is the representative of my power. Khalsa will do well. The mother then went away. Here ends the 26th Sakhee.

SAKHEE TWENTY-SEVENTH.

In the last hours of the night, in which the Gooroo's mother had the conversation mentioned in the 26th Sakhee the Seikhs heard that Saida Khan Puthan was approaching near them with the army of 1,25,000 men. The Seikhs reported to the Gooroo that the Moghul and Puthan army was encamped at Thunesur and that they will attack the Seikhs to-morrow. The Gooroo said, O Khalsa there are five hundred Seikhs only and the forces of the Rajahs are on the opposite side, you may fight if you can. Before it was morning the armies arrived. Memo Khan Puthan, an offier in the Gooroo's service having 100 men under his command spoke out, O King, I have eaten your salt, see my bravery to day! The Gooroo then granted him a bow and said, go, it is better to kill the equals. The battle raged in the morning between Khalsa and Rajah's forces The Khalsa reported to the Gooroo that the military stores were greatly wanting. The Gooroo ordered them to shut their eyes. They did so, and saw millions of Seikh forces around them and all the stones and sand appeared as gun-powder, lead gun-balls, bullets, arrows and quivers. The Seikhs were pleased and shone with valour. The Gooroo sat on a small hillock and began to inspect the battle. The battle raged and each one of the Seikhs was attacked by hundreds of Mahammedans. The battle was fought with guns, swords, daggers and arrows. The officers of the Gooroo's army, viz., brave Sahib Singh, Run Singh, Dya Singh, Dhurm Singh, Tham Sing and Beer Singh, fought with the chiefs of the Mahammedan army. Saida Khan had previously heard of the magnificent appearance of the Gooroo and was, therefore, secretly anxious to have a view of the Gooroo, to whom he could not go openly, being afraid of the other Mahammedans. The Gooroo miraculously knowing of his anxiety, girdled himself and mounting on horse-back harangued Saida Khan, saying, Beware! O Khan jee, uphold your arms! Saida Khan made salam to the Gooroo with folded hands and said, "I have seen the true God in the shape of man, truly and exactly the Lord of his believers"! The Gooroo said O Khan jee, it is the duty of officer to view the battle. The Khan then fell upon Gooroo's feet, became a devotee and went away. No one knew where he had gone to, Rumzan Begh seeing this fell upon the Gooroo, who killed him with an arrow. The Khalsa then fled, fighting as they retired. The Gooroo's camp was plundered by the Mahammedans, who were outwardly pleased but felt afraid in their hearts. The Mahammedan camp then returned to Surbund on the next day, and the

Seikhs rejoined the Gooroo and said, O king, after conquering, you made us to be defeated. Give us orders even now. The Gooroo said, O Seikhs I am not free in my will, but am subject to the will of some other person,[1] as you are subject to the will of mine. The Gooroo then repeated the following verses, *viz.*, "Even the sun and moon are in fears. Notwithstanding their travelling over millions of miles they find no end, &c., &c., &c." The Gooroo said Moghuls and Puthans will be defeated up to Dehlie. The Khalsa moved the next day and plundered the Mahammedan camp on the road to Shumsabad. The defeated fled and reached Dehlie. Aurungzeb heard this and was sorry. He sighed deeply, shook his head and began to repent. Here ends the 27th Sakhee.

SAKHEE TWENTY-EIGHT.

On the next day Aurungzeb called a counsel of all his chiefs, wise men, Kazees and those who were defeated in the last battle and asked them, what tumult has the Hindoo caused? What is the number of his army and what amount of bravery he has? Who helps him that he has become a guide of the human beings? The courtiers replied that he is so generous as to spend lakh of Rupees in the place of one Rupee, that he is very clever and of young age, that he is the chief and the living Peer and that he is the lord of the helpless creatures. Aurungzeb said, "I will restore Mahammedans again to power and will destroy those who praise, belong to, or are well-wishers of the Hindoos. But how shall I proceed now, he is not my equal nor belongs to the beloved religion." Hearing this the Kazee said, "O Sir, let us call him amicably and see what sort of person he is. This opinion was approved of by all and "Purwanas" were issued to the Gooroo to

---

[1] Meaning God.

the effect that there is only one empire and you agree with us in religious sentiments, so better come here to see us. If you would not come I will meet you with the army and your reputation as a devotee will be injured. You may live in my kingdom as other saints and devotees." To this were added some haughty words as usual with the style of royal Purwanas and a sentence that he (Aurungzeb) had the kingdom granted to him by the true God. Some ambassadors were sent with these letters to the Gooroo, who received them civilly and after giving them present dismissed them, sending with them two of his principal men, viz., Dya Singh of Lahore and Dhurm Singh of Agra, with the letter the contents of which were as follows, "O Aurungzeb Emperor, thou wishest to try devotees supernatural power. Being void of all goodness, what answer will you give in the presence of the Great God, who is the Lord of all religions. Akber, Alexander, Hoomayoon and their ancestors and the lords of Bulkt and China, were reduced to ashes and blown away by the wind. All haughty and proud are at last puffed off by the wind. You have not made your heart pure even one day. The way of God is holy and fearless. You do not know the value and merit of purity." The Gooroo then by means of his words granted his own courage and power to the above-named Seikhs, who departed and reached Aurungzeb's Court. Aurungzeb by means of his miraculous powers used to go to Mecca every day. In order to humble his pride the Gooroo also one day girdled himself and miraculously arrived in Mecca. When Aurungzeb finished his worship the Gooroo threatened him from within saying, "who are you?" Saying this the Gooroo drove Aurungzeb before him and taking him on a hill made him stand on a high platform among his courtiers, who were also present there. Aurungzeb being afraid of the Gooroo stood there. A voice was heard from a distance saying, "O creature, be careful not to see [1] the countenance of the Gooroo again. I am the Gooroo and the Gooroo is I, you are a creature do not try to be equal to me." The voice further directed the Gooroo to let Aurungzeb go and then the Gooroo at the recommendation of courtiers allowed Aurungzeb to go. A little after this the Gooroo made over his quiver to "Aurungzeb" and told him to keep it and to send it to the Gooroo whenever he asks for it. Aurungzeb then awaked and trembled. In the morning after ablutions the Emperor held his Court and sent for Dya Singh and Dhurm Singh, the ambassadors of the Gooroo. They came in, and delivering the letter, saluted the emperor on behalf of the Gooroo with the words, "Futtah [2] Wah gooroojee kee." The Seikhs at the time of saluting looked towards the Gooroo's letter, as if it were they were saluting the latter and not the Mahammedan emperor and thus proved them strong faith in Seikhism. Aurungzeb was silent at this, and caused the letter to be read out, wherein it was secretly recorded, "give me my deposit." Aurungzeb then asked the ambassadors, who are you"? They replied, we, are Gooroo's Seikh," He asked, "where is the Gooroo,"? they said "the Gooroo is before you." He asked, "do you possess miraculous powers"? they said, "Gooroo's *dogs even* possess miraculous powers." The emperor said, "give me one dog of this sort." Dya Singh sent for a hound from his dwelling and made it stand before the Emperor. The dog uttered his voice and said, "If you will separate yourself from our species you will remain in trouble, come to me, you do not possess reason like men." The Emperor understood it and was ashamed. He dismissed his courtiers and then said, what! Has Khalsa come to existence? Why have they flourished in my reign? Dya Singh, hearing this said,

---

[1] i. e. Do not call him in your Court..

[2] Salutation of the Seikhs, meaning "Victory to the blessed Gooroo."

you also have been too hasty in making one religion throughout the world. The Gooroo has established the 3rd religion, viz., Seikhism, as separate from Hindooism, and Mahammedanism. The emperor then asked, " what is your Gooroo doing ? Dya Singh said, " he is collecting arms, and has asked back the weapon deposited with you. The Emperor then ordered the quiver to be brought. Royal servants attended and brough the quiver. The Emperor then said that he considered the Gooroo as brother or of equal position with him, and asked Dya Singh, whether he had seen the Gooroo with his own eyes. Dya Sing replied that he had seen the Gooroo wearing his arms and fighting in battles, that he is a hero undoubtedly. The emperor said, he will make soldiers of all his subjects. Dya Singh said, God will send mysterious armies and the 10th true king will come on the day of battle. The emperor then dismissed the Seikh ambassadors after delivering his letter to them for the Gooroo. The principal contents of the letter were this, " I of course appeared humble in Mecca, but there will be much disgrace of Khalsa in fighting against me, I will not persecute my subjects, but Khalsa will be more and more disgraced every day." The ambassadors then arrived and delivered the letter with the presents and the quiver. The Seikhs enquired about the quiver and the Gooroo ordered Dya Singh to explain it to them. Here ends the 28th Sakhee.

SAKHEE TWENTY-NINTH.

Once a Seikh came and begged before the Gooroo, saying, O true king, I am disgusted with the world, lead me to peace and deliver me from the pains of births and deaths. I have sought your protection, save me from sins. I am not educated. The Gooroo said, blessed are you O Seikh brother, in whose mind hatred to the world is created, but a man without learning, can understand nothing, therefore, it is necessary to learn more or less. An illiterate man walks like a blind person and cannot understand anything, whose words are right, he finds God. So you should read O brother. The Gooroo then recommended him to a learned Seikh, whom he ordered to teach the young Seikh with love. The teacher took the young Seikh with him and began to teach him. The first thing he read was the following verse of Anundjee :—" Extremely happy, I have become O my mother, I have found the true Gooroo." Having read this verse the young Seikh went away to his dwelling, and never came to read again, but continued to eat from the Gooroo's Lunger now and then. The meaning of the above verse imparted faith in him. After six months the Gooroo asked the teacher whether the young Seikh had learned something. The teacher said he only read one verse and never came again to read. The Gooroo sent for him and told him, O Seikh, I had sent you to read! The young Seikh said with folded hands, O Gooroo one verse is sufficient, " I became extremely happy when I found the Gooroo." To read more beyond this is the work of faithless. The Gooroo was pleased and laughing said, blessed art thou O Seikh, thou hast been emancipated from the bondage of births and deaths. Here ends the 29th Sakhee.

SAKHEE THIRTIETH.

Once the people mere discoursing on theological subjects, when the Gooroo put the following question, *viz.*, In whose reign did "Kubeer" live? The old persons in the company spoke out to reply to this question. Some said, Hoomayoon was the king of that time, others said Puthowra. Few said Alexander and a certain number said Mudanpal the king of Jaines. The question was discussed for a long time, but no truth was found out. The

Gooroo heard all this, and then read the following verse, "We cannot reach the Godly-men, they are very high, castes, tribes and kingdoms are all below them." All the persons became silent and the Seikhs asked O true king, why had you asked this question, you better answer this. The Gooroo replied, O Seikhs such is the excellence of God's Name! The Kings who possess millions of wealth, are unknown, but see the greatness of God; in Kubeer's age there were thousands of famous Pundits,[1] Astronomers Rich men, kings, but no one knows of them; but through the glory of God's name Kubeer is known to all, as possessing full knowledge of God and having the power of miracles. Blessed is the Name of God! O Seikhs. The Alexander with all his pomp and glory of conquering India, had paid homage to the Kubeer as soon as he had known of his miraculous power. O Seikhs whoever will remember the Name of God will be the true Seikh of the Gooroo. The best precept is to remember God's name and to serve the human beings. Here ends the 30th Sakhee.

SAKHEE THIRTY-FIRST.

Once when the Gooroo was sitting in a Hall, a Seikh asked him, "what is the easiest way of salvation?" adding that the way pointed out by the Shasters and Pundits is the most difficult one. The Gooroo said, "it is very easy to obtain salvation. Leave the cares of the world. Make the mind peaceful, the truth which is hidden like a butterfly in her feathers will be discovered. Repeat the name of "Ram" (God) and remember death. The first will destroy your past sins and the latter will enable you to abstain from committing sins, in future." Here ends the 31st Sakhee.

[1] Learned in Sanskrit literature.

SAKHEE THIRTY-SECOND.

Once a Seikh was taken captive by Mahammedans, who circumcised him, made him to eat with them, forced him to read Kulma, shaved off the long hairs of his head and converted him to Mahammedan faith according to ceremonies of their religion. The Seikh, however, remained faithful to his own religion in his mind and repeated the name of Gooroo in his heart. The Mahammedans after completely turning him to their faith, dismissed him. In the evening when "Rowhrass," was being read, that Seikh came before the Gooroo and bending his head spoke out, O true king, I am a Seikh. I fell down senseless while fighting in a battle and was taken captive by Mahammedans, who according to the ceremonies of their religion converted me to Mahammedanism. Now, what shall I do? Restore me to Hindooism and Seikhism as you like, otherwise I will burn myself alive. The Gooroo said what ceremonies did they perform at the time of converting you? The Seikh related all that had passed. The Gooroo then asked him, whether he had enjoyed a Mahammedan woman. The Seikh replied, No Sir, you saved me from such a sin. The Gooroo then ordered him to prepare Karah prashad and to distribute it to the Seikhs. You are a real Seikh, the Gooroo has protected you. The Seikhs who were present on that occasion asked, O true king, how does a man become Mahammedan or is it impossible to become a Mahammedan? The Gooroo replied no one can be made Mahammedan by force, for the enemies always use such a force to spoil the religion; but when a man being filled with lust enjoys a Mahammedan woman, his mind is affected and thus he becomes a Mahammedan. Mind is the chief cause of all, no one can turn its belief by force. Whoever even once enjoys a Mahammedan woman, is not my Seikh. A Hindoo should always abstain from enjoying a Mahammedan woman. One who commits adultery with another man's wife and does afterwards repent and atone for it, or causes himself to be forgivèn by Gooroo's Seikhs, he will be saved But one who enjoys a Mahammedan woman, is a complete Mahammedan and can never be forgiven. If any one unknowing and ignorantly enjoys a Mahammedan woman, but afterwards becomes a Seikh, he is also forgiven. The Seikhs then asked, O true king, the Mahammedans enjoy the Hindoo women, so what a good it is if the Seikhs, to revenge them, may enjoy Mahammedan women. Why have the Gooroo and the Shasters forbidden this. The Gooroo said O Seikhs, I want to raise this sect higher and not to throw down. Mahammed is the prophet of goblins, therefore we should not imitate the mean fellows. It is proper for the Gooroo to obey the precepts of "Shasters" with reference to castes. Here ends the 32nd Sakhee.

SAKHEE THIRTY-THIRD.

Once the Gooroo had celebrated the "Holy"[1] festival. The godly and devotional Seikhs made a long and wonderful job of it. They made many sorts of funs, such as singing, music, mimicries and other merry sports of several kinds, to show the Gooroo, who examined the curious performances of the world. After the Hola ceremony was over, the people of the assembly told him, O true king, how splendidly this festival has been celebrated! But in this fair the wives of two Seikhs have eloped. The Gooroo said, such things always happen in fairs, the only good thing in it that we can see is the countenances of several godly persons. There are many persons, who assemble at the sacred institutions, festivals and death-ceremonies, but very few of them obtain the fruits of goodness. O Seikhs the Gooroo is always pleased alike.

---

[1] Hola or Holee.

If we are not to live in this world, why should we daub ourselves in mud ? O Brother, if we are to die, why should we be proud ? Those who have a taste of Heavenly things, do not prefer any of the worldly things. The Gooroo's Durbar is like a looking-glass, which reflects the true features of the thing put before it and does not partake of the sorrow or pleasure of the reflected object, such is the manner of the Gooroo. Whoever serves him with good intention obtains good fruits and whoever serves him with evil intention gets evil fruits. Looking at this point of view, we can say that the ancestors of Hindoos have established bad customs for their posterity, while Mahammedans have established good ones for their followers. For the latter weep on their sacred days and say, "we cannot behave as virtuously as our ancestors did. We are negligent O God, protect us and forgive us" ! While the former on their festivals such as, "Holy," "Lahree," "Dewalee," &c. rejoice, become merry and males and females of them address each other with lustful and obscene words. O Seikhs devotional beings are the happiest beings in both worlds, others being bound like beasts in the ceremonies of their respective religions die and are reborn over and over again. O Seikh brothers, no one can be saved without virtue and devotion. The God is not pleased by laughings and merry jumps. The people will repent after death. The blind man will know when it falls on his head. O Seikhs neither the Krishn, nor Bishn, nor Ram saves. But when this man will understand *himself,* then his worship and devotions will come in account. Here ends the 33rd Sakhee.

SAKHEE THIRTY-FOURTH.

Once the Gooroo was seated on a hillock and was crowded all around by the people. A Seikh woman with a veil before her face came several times to see the Gooroo, but finding him crowded returned again. The Gooroo observed her and sent for her. The male relations were already sitting there. She bent her head and stood before the Gooroo with covered face. The Gooroo said, Well! O Seikh woman, say! the Gooroo knows you already, but it is necessary to reveal it to the Suugat. The Seikh woman with folded hands said, O true king, my parents were the residents of Raipoor. When I was a virgin an old devotee came to our house and my parents served him diligently. He lived five years in our house. I used to serve him and to hear the contents of the sacred Books (Shasters and Vedas) from him. After this I was married to a young Khutree of Bursana, whose wife I am. My husband is also a godly man and receives Seikhs and devotees with hospitality. I prepare food for such persons with love and eagerness and obtain their good will and pleasure. There is mutual love between me and my husband, whom I consider as my Lord and Gooroo, for I had heard from the devotee that husband is the protector of the wife. My father-in-law, husband and his brothers and sons and their wives used to go for obtaining, "Durshun" of the Gooroos, but I, the wretched, never obtained your "Durshun," saying to my mind, "who will serve the Seikh guests in my absence?" My relatives, however, brought me here though not agreeable to my husband's wish. Though I am come here, but my attention is still fixed in my cooking duties. When I saw the Gooroo crowded I turned back saying to myself, "I am a sinner! how can I obtain the Gooroo's "Durshun?" I should go back and attend to my cooking duties." In the meanwhile Your Seikh came to me and told me O Seikh woman, you are called by the Gooroo. I was then pleased. You have been kind to me, O Gooroo, please order me what should I do now? The Gooroo said, blessed art thou O Seikh woman and blessed are thy parents and the persons of thy husband's family, that you on hearing once only, have proved faithful to your husband and in serving devotees. I will also give some present to you when your husband will come. Go for the present O Devi, your desire is fulfilled, remain in the house and continue in serving the devotees. This is the right way of finding the Gooroo. Here ends the 34th Sakhee.

SAKHEE THIRTY-FIFTH.

On the next day the above-mentioned Seikh woman came to the Gooroo with her husband. The Gooroo asked her, O Seikh woman whose wife you are? She felt ashamed and said, "had the Gooroo been ignorant, I might have told him, but the Gooroo knows all his Sungat." The Gooroo then asked the accompanying Seikh whether she was his wife. The Seikh replied, I do not consider any thing mine, the body, mind and wealth all belong to the Gooroo, even our own body, which is so closely connected with the soul, does not remain. I am therefore, the dust of the feet of the Seikhs of Seikhs. The Gooroo said, O Seikh you do not know, but shall know hereafter. O Seikh in your previous birth you were Kubeer Bhuggut[1] and this Seikh woman was "Loi."[2] You one day said her, O Loi, what have you earned in this life. She said she had yet an eager desire for serving the godly men. The Kubeer said, this is not the way in which a wife should behave, she should always abide by her husband's will. Go and be born in a Khutree's house. You shall have faith in Baba Nanuk's religion, and will obtain salvation through the Gooroo's words and "Durshuns."[3] The Loi then fell upon Kubeer's feet and begged of him not to leave her in that birth also. Kubeer said O Godly woman as your desire is only to serve the

[1] Godly man.
[2] The wife of Kubeer.
[3] Seeing, look.

holy men, I also agree to take another birth. The Gooroo continued, O Seikh you have now forgotten yourself, for the past age was a good one, but now no one awakes unless the Gooroo awakens him. Saying this the Gooroo gave them " Karah Prashad" to eat. When they ate it their mind was supernaturally enlightened, and they happened to know of their previous births. They entreated the Gooroo and solicited for his further orders. The Gooroo said when the precepts and poetries of the " Grunth Sahib[1] " were collected, you had appeared without body, but now you have appeared to me in human body ; read to me some of the verses made by Kubeer, that the Seikhs may believe it. The husband of that Seikh woman then read the verses. The Gooroo then informed other Seikhs that Kubeer was the chief of all devotees and that the Gooroo has also approved of his doctrines, which are spread in all the Seikhs. The Gooroo wants to guard the Hindoo faith in Kuliyoga, hence he has established this religion. The Seikh woman and her husband, being awakened went to their house and applied themselves to worship and to the work of serving the Seikhs according to the Gooroo's word. Here ends the 35th Sakhee.

SAKHEE THIRTY-SIXTH.

Once Deena Begh Moghul, as induced by Rajah Bheem Chund, Muddenpal, Beer Singh, Juspalia and Surmoria, marched against the Gooroo with 10,000 horse. A dreadful battle was fought in the presence of the Sungat who were also assembled at that time. The Gooroo mounted on his blue horse and wearing his quiver and sword engaged himself in war on the banks of a rivulet, on the other side of which was the Mahammedan army.

---

[1] The famous Book of the Seikhs.

The guns fired, swords played and the bows cracked. The Seikhs weighed the battle and killed many of the Toorks. Another force of the Mahammedans followed, from which a "Puthan" archer named Painde Khan wearing an armour and proud of his skill in arrows came out and harangued, saying, "we are to fight for the sake of religion, your Gooroo is powerful, let us fight! Hearing this the Gooroo went forward and spoke, O Khan, you are my old enemy, come then, make the 1st attack and show your hands. The Puthan said you are a prophet of the Hindoos, show your hands first, for you shall not be saved from my arrow. I shall reduce you to dust by my awful arrow. The Gooroo said one who first harangued should make the first attack. The Puthan then prepared and while all were eagerly looking, turned his horse in a circle around the Gooroo, discharged an arrow, which forcibly passed by one of the ears of the Gooroo. The Gooroo asked the "khan" to make another attack but he felt ashamed. However upon the Gooroo's repeatedly saying so, the Puthan said heroes only make one attack, but according to your word I make another. Saying this angrily discharged another arrow, which passed through the shawl bound on the Gooroo's head. The Khan stood silent and the Gooroo asked the permission to attack him according to the turn. The Khan allowed the Gooroo to attack him twice. The Gooroo said heroes only make one attack. Two attacks are made but by foolish and wicked persons. Saying this the Gooroo went round the Puthan and observed that no place of his body was unprotected but an ear, at which he therefore shoot with an arrow. The Puthan fell down from his horse, when the Gooroo drew his sword and came upon the head of the Puthan, who exclaimed, "Save me O Gooroo." The Gooroo said, O Puthan this is not the time of saving, repeat your "Kulma." Saying this the Gooroo cut off his head and defeated the Mahammedan army. Great plunder was made and the drums of victory sounded. The Seikhs were victorious and shouted victory ! victory ! The Khalsa fell upon the rest of the Mahammedan army and plundering them reached Khidrabad village. Here ends the 36th Sakhee.

SAKHEE THIRTY-SEVENTH.

On a certain occasion many of the Seikhs were killed in battle. The Gooroo was besieged in the Anundpoor and all the Hill Rajas had leagued against him. Fifteen days after the seige, the Gooroo set out to fight, but all the Seikhs had been hungry since many days, on account of their having been besieged for 15 days, and the supplies from outside having been prevented at that time. The Gooroo in order to try the Khalsa's faith ordered his treasures to be thrown into the Sutlej River. The Seikhs began to starve and cried out O Gooroo save us ! The Seikhs notwithstanding their feeling the pains of starvation did not cease to fight, on the contrary determined to die at the feet of the Gooroo. One day Mai Goojree said to the Gooroo, what ! thou art called a Gooroo and are making arrangements to kill your Seikhs, who are fighting battles for you. The enemy is approaching too quickly, our Seikhs are starving and you are causing the stores to be thrown into the Sutlej river ! How will these men fight ! What sin have they committed that they are made to starve ! ! They get only about 1½ chitak of gram to eat as their daily food. Please forgive, and be kind to your Seikhs. The Gooroo replied, this religion has been established by the order of God, I wish to increase and not to destroy it. Why they will eat out of the proceeds of religious offerings from which our Treasures are provided, they will begin to diminish, for, O mother, the food obtained from such proceeds is poisonous in its effects. I have created this sect for military purposes, they are better off while suffering from hunger and want of clothes. But I will not let them go to hell nor will deceive them. As you O my mother, cannot give me poison to eat, so I cannot allow these persons to eat from the proceeds of religious offerings. I will now commit these stores as deposit to Sutlej River, which will purify them by course of time, as the poison reduced to ashes, by proper preparations, becomes a medicine and can by its effect cure several sorts of diseases. When in the sumbut 1899 Hindee, Duleep Singh my Seikh will come into existence, we will retake this our deposit from the Sutlej River. The Khalsa will then make tour towards the east. The wicked will hide themselves in the Hills. The silent Englishmen and "Mourjee" of bad caste will join the Khalsa and will hold counsels together. The Khalsa will then break up. There shall be friendship between Hindoos, Mahammedans, Moulvees, Englishmen and Soonees.[1] The Khalsa will again become powerful and will then conquer the English or English will conquer the Mahammedans. All the villages will be broken and the people will be in distress. The country shall be empty of justice. The Seikh women will practice as prostitutes and will be waiting for Mahammedan whoremongers and will become polluted by the Mahammedans. At such a time the Khalsa will again arise and will restore the people to their respective faiths. The mother hearing these words remained silent and stopped the persons from throwing treasure into the river, saying, be ceased! O servant, the money is dear to my mother, she would not let the nation increase. Here ends the 37th Sakhee.

SAKHEE THIRTY-EIGHTH.

Once the Gooroo fought with the Hill-Rajahs. Great noise was caused by the sounds of kettle-drums, large

[1] A Division of Mahammedans.

drums, trumpets, cornets, clarions, drums &c. &c. The Gooroo retreated and the worthless Hill-men plundered the camp horses, clothes, carriages and wealth were all plunderd. The Seikhs began to weep and cry and said, "The Gooroo is put to much loss, how shall we win! The Gooroo's endless wealth has been plundered, how shall we reach home! We feel ashamed to go to our houses, for we could not defend the Gooroo's treasures." Their cries rent the sky! The Gooroo ordered the Seikhs to draw lines on the ground with their fingers and then to rule them off. The Gooroo then asked whether they had been pleased or sorry in drawing and rubbing the lines. The Seikhs replied, O true king we felt neither pleased nor sorry. The Gooroo said likewise I do not feel pleasure or sorrow in seeing myself put to loss or in finding my income decreased or increased. This world is the place of sorrow. In a moment we become happy and in another moment sorry. Whoever awakes (*i. e.* remembers God) is in peace, but those who are in opposite condition, are mournful and suffering pains. Remember God's name and always think upon the meanings of the Gooroo's words. Those who are instructed in Gooroo's words do not become sorry. If the woman who bathes very carefully and adorns herself with 16 sorts[1] of embellishments, is not loved and liked by her husband, all becomes useless to her and she gains nothing thereby but shame. One who has come into the world under the name of Gooroo, has no ambition whatever. He only is the true Seikh, who submits to the Gooroo's will. Hearing this all the Seikhs were restored to peace. On the next day the Gooroo again kindly ordered that whoever will fight and will not fly back, shall be my real Seikh. A dreadful fighting then ensued. Here ends the 38th Sakhee.

---

[1] Customary in Indian ladies.

SAKHEE THIRTY-NINTH.

Once Pumma Wuzeer[1] of Macbur Got[2] was sent by Rajah Bheem to the Gooroo to negotiate for peace and he arriving at the Gooroo's camp addressed him, saying, We have known it surely that you are the true and king Gooroo! The Gooroo replied O Pumma Wuzeer at last Bepeer,[3] (meaning thereby that you will be faithless at last) the words of Brahman, without being fully understood are like colick. Persons of Rajpoot family are not faithful even to their parents and devotees. The clothes if stained with a drop of blood, become impure, but the blood if drunk,[4] Baba Nanuk says, makes the human mind pure and holy. The Pumma hearing this said it is not good to reject the application of one, who seeks for protection. In the meantime all the sodhees and seikhs, who were present on the occasion recommended the terms of friendship, saying it is not proper to continue fighting every day. The Gooroo then spoke out saying, that, completely good is Rajpoot's family in which enemies are always born. They kill their fathers and cut off the heads of their friend's sons. Hill men are never good. Trust them very carefully. When they are in difficulty, they become Fakeers (beggars) and deceive their father. When they are well provided with corn and milk, they begin to worship "Devtas." They make friendship with one, whom they find to be rich and with whom they have some business. They talk affectionately and pityfully, but are not so in mind. They pretend to be faithful to both parties at enmity with each other, and prefer eating than taking, and keep themselves distant from a person who is in trouble. The Gooroo then said to his sungat, you can make friendship with these men if you like, but I would not advise it.

---

1 Prime Minister.

2 Subdivision of a caste.

3 Literally having no spiritual guide but the meaning here given is "faithless."

4 Drinking one's own blood is to lead a rigid devotional life.

Saying this, the Gooroo kept quiet and the Pumma began to live in the seikh's Camp. Being a wise man Pumma gained interest in the seikh assembly and the Gooroo himself began to trust in him. Pumma then secretly informed his Rajah that he had succeeded in earning the Gooroo's trust and good will towards him. Now[1] Pumma began to show his faith in the Gooroo. First of all he caused the Gooroo's best horses to be stolen and privately estimated all his treasures. No one knew this secret except the Gooroo and all believed him to be a good seikh. He secretly invited Mahammedan armies to attack the Gooroo and sent for the forces of his own Rajah evidently with the view of assisting the Gooroo, but secretly to act against him. He never disclosed the secrecies of his mind and publicly served the Gooroo to show his faith, like a thief. Here ends the 39th Sakhee.

SAKHEE FORTIETH.

Once the Gooroo went out for hunting, Rajpoots took him very far and showed him the fun of killing lions. They took their meals together and ate the flesh of sword slain animals. Many days were thus passed, when the fair of Rewalsur drew near. The Pumma[2] asked the Gooroo to go to Rewalsur at the approaching fair, saying, that he will happen to see many Rajahs there, who might become his Seikhs. The Gooroo was acquainted with his evil intentions but at the recommendation of the Sungat accepted his proposal. At that time one Mudden Sing Chumar,[3] who was groom of Gooroo's horse, uttered the following words, " Whoever will do evil, wlll reap the results of it. What harm can any one do to the Gooroo! His servants will at last discharge their duties and the enemy will die

---

[1] Ironically.

[2] Well known in the previous Sakhee.

[3] A shoe-maker by caste.

while at a distance" The seikhs hearing these words muttered among themselves, What does this groom say ! Mudden Sing groom hearing this laughed and became silent. The Gooroo said, O Brethern this man has been a servant of my horse for 12 months. Serving Gooroo's horse is as good as serving a cow. Whoever will serve Gooroo's horse without a desire of worldly profits, will be master of the knowledge of Vedas and Shasters. The Gooroo then said to Mudden Singh groom, serve the horse well ! and digest what reward[1] you have obtained ! This is Gooroo's house, its protector is Sutgoor or the true God. Be silent O Seikh, and calmly pass the days of silence. Saying this the Gooroo went away. Many Hill Rajahs with their armies were gathered at Rewalsur, such as, Chumbal, Bhugial, Mudonea, Siree-Nugria, Kamgurhia, Hindour, Kulour, Ghoomund Chund and Moodel. All the Rajpoot Rajahs came to see the Gooroo and were charmed by seeing him, for he was both beautiful in appearance and excellent in qualities. All the Rajahs and Queens were saying, "We have found the Gooroo corresponding with the good fame spread abroad about him." Some were saying, "Blessed are the Rajpoot kings, who have had the pleasure of the interview with the Gooroo." After sacred ablution, prayer and devotions, the Gooroo seated himself on a hillock and was seen by the virgin daughter of the Chumbal Rajah, who was a poetess. She asked the permission of her father to write to the Gooroo, as she always delighted in reading Gooroo's poetries and said to herself that the words of Gooroo's verses are not fine though the meanings are excellent and charming. She was, therefore, anxious to to see the Gooroo. She then wrote a letter to the Gooroo, in which first she praised him very much and at last put the following 4* questions to him and solicited their answer.

---

[1] Meaning the power of foresight or miraculous power.

* In fact 3 questions.

1 What is complete and what is incomplete?

2 Who is the constant attendant with the man and where do men and women roam?

3 What do we eat and with what do we sleep?

Boodha Sahib says, that in his presence the Gooroo wrote the following answers instantly, "O Princess, these are answers to your questions."

1st Devta's body is complete and man's incomplete.

2nd Cares of the world are constant attendants with the man and men and women roam in the two worlds after death.

3rd Men are eating or enjoying the fruits of their good or bad actions and at the time of universal destruction they sleep with their sins or virtues.

Reading these answers the Rajah's daughter procured her father's permission and went to pay her respects to the Gooroo, who at the time of bending her head before him, touched[1] her back with the point of her bow. The Rajah's daughter then asked the Gooroo, why hast thou touched me with a bow and not by hand? The Gooroo replied in last birth you were Aurungzeb's wife and had caused an Inn to be built on a River ferry, by virtue of which, you have obtained this body. Now as it is prohibited for a seikh to touch Mahammedan woman and considering you late enemy, I have not touched you but on account of the faith you put in me, I grant you the birth of the holy place "Dumduma Sahib." You shall at the end of this life be born there and become the wife of "Dulla Choudree." You shall in that birth serve the seikh's males and females and I will grant my "Durshun[2]" to you at that time.

---

[1] A sign of accepting the compliments and imparting blessings.

[2] Interview.

The Gooroo bestowed this favor on her, she led a holy and religious life and after her death was born in "Malwa." Here ends the 40th Sakhee.

SAKHEE FORTY-FIRST.

At a certain time the Gooroo accompained with five seikhs ascended on Molvhee hill, and was met there with a Ghundheela,[1] who bowed his head before the Gooroo. "What have you understood of me," said the Gooroo, "that you have bowed your head before me. The Gundheela laughing replied" that I am the son of "Reva" and am, therefore, called by the name of "Reval." At my mother's advice I had devoted myself to divine meditations and in the country of Outor khund[2] "spent 3 yogs[3] in such devotions. At the end of these sacred labours Brahma[4] appeared before me. I praised him in songs, whereupon he said, O son of Nag,[5] ask whatever you desire and I will give it to you. I told him that I have a desire for the enjoyments of imperial grandeur. Brahma said to me "stop" and at the same instant ordered "Wissokurma[6]" to build a city, which was named Mundup, I become the king of that city and reigned 63 yogs, after which the Yakhs[7] took away the kingdom from me and I was slain in the battle. The place of my worship became a "Teeruth[8]" by the order of Brahma. I will remain here till the time of "Nihkalunk[9] Autar," finding you who are also an incarnate hero, on this Hill, I have placed

---

[1] A spiritual being of mean caste.

[2] Or Northern Division of India.

[3] One of the famous four eras of Hindoo mythology.

[4] One of the three Hindoo gods.

[5] A rational race of serpents in Hindoo mythology, who talk like human beings.

[6] Chief Engineer of Gods in Hindoo mythology.

[7] Spiritual beings of middle caste said to abound in Budree Narain Hills of Himalaya Range.

[8] A sacred place of Hindoo pilgrimage.

[9] One of the incarnations of deity, who will flourish in the end, of Kuliyog or modern era.

myself under your protection. Advise the Yakhs to be at good terms with me and, O Gooroo, protect me." The Gooroo then drew his bow and the Hills began to tremble and exclaimed,—"O Gooroo save us." In the meanwhile a man wearing deer-skin with long matted hair on the head and small hair all over the body came and thus spoke to the Gooroo,—"O Gooroo, your time of coming here has not yet arrived, be pleased to go now—Whenever your religion will spread you will come to the yakhs also. I am a faithful yakh—we always fight with Nags.—You should assist both parties and we will give you an army of 10,000 soldiers when at the time of spreading your religion you will come to our house." The Gooroo said although the army of Toorks[1] is numberless I can destroy them all with one arrow. But I should act according to the fashion of Kuliyoga. In the meanwhile Rawul spoke, "O, Father, I will come to you with an army of a Karor[2] of horrible serpents, viz. Akálees[3] in the sumbut 99. I will then conquer "Gundhurb Des" or the country of Kundhar for you and establish your religion in the field of battle. I will reduce the Toorks to utter destruction. The light shall exist for 50 years—it will be all quiet and tranquility. The descendants of "Kupees[4] Gundhurb," viz., Englishmen will occupy the country of Mahammedans. So I will drive them out and will allow your religion to remain. My glory will extend. I will produce two sons from "Mudna" woman and will then divide the world by the force of fighting. There shall be one kingdom from Kamgurh, Piryag and Dehlie up to the east. The other will reign over Sindh territory, Ravi, Chunder, Bhoga, and Sutlej up to Kashmeer and will be called *Almi*[5]. Saying this Rawal prepared himself to accom-

[1] Mahammedans.
[2] 10,000,000.
[3] A fanatic seikh soldiery.
[4] A heavenly being supposed to be governor of monkeys.
[5] Owner of the Alum or world.

pany the Gooroo, who told him, O Brother, you go to Koober and tell him that after fighting battles, establishing the true religion, creating religious enmity with the Mahammedans and destroying Aurungzeb I will go towards the south. Rawul was pleased and told the Gooroo :—"You shall have a calamity of one year, when I will meet you. The "Gayutree[1]" was displeased with with you on account of your establishing the ceremony of "Pahul" and thus despising her. She, therefore, cursed you to one years' calamity. So be careful! I will come to assist you every now and then. Sakhee 41st finished.

SAKHEE FORTY-SECOND.

Once all the Sungat were gathered together and were offering presents to the Gooroo, Ardasia was reading prayers of acceptance and the treasurer was receiving the money. Some gave pices, some Rupees and some gold Mohurs. Few gave in hundreds, others in thousands &c. Thus a large treasure was collected, and the seikhs were obtaining the asked for desires from the Gooroo. At that time one "Kazee" "Solar Deen" was also present there. He was a godly man and had no animosity with the Gooroo. When the crowd was away he asked, "why do your seikhs pay you presents, while the Brahmans say that it happens whatever God does and you Hindoos say that all things are ordained by the God from the 1st day. We Mahammedans have also a similar belief. Who is it that can upset God's doings! So tell me what is your belief, for you who are able to give the sons and fortune to the people, will not lie. The Gooroo then told him hear O respected Kazee! and took off his seal-ring from off his finger and sealed it on a paper, after which

[1] The principal Munter or miraculous verse of the Brahmans, here it is personified and is meant by the goddess of that verse.

said, O Kazee, when this man is created, his fate is engraved on his forehead but remains reverse as letters on the seal, and when he bends his head before the Gooroo or Peer, his fate becomes straight as the letters of the seal become straight when impressed on paper. The Engraver[1] of the letters of fortune, engraved the reverse letters on the forehead of the man and told him O man, these letters will become straight when you will bend your head before the Gooroo, if not these letters will remain reverse as they are. So, for this reason, the Gooroo continued Seikhs become purified in putting their faith in the Gooroo. Hearing this the Kazee made "Salam"[2] to the Gooroo and said O true King by your favor I have overcome the world. The Kazee again exclaimed Wah![3] Wah! The true God that I have found, in the first stage, is the Gooroo, who has made the servant of his feet, cross the ocean of the world. Here ends the 42nd Sakhee.

SAKHEE FORTY-THIRD.

Once all the Sungat were assembled around the Gooroo and were obtaining the desires of their heart from him, when the Gooroo said, Is there any such woman, who should have never cursed a minor or grown up man? A Seikh woman out of the assembly said with her folded hands, O true king, I have never done so nor have I ever chided my own son. The Gooroo said O Seikh daughter, how may I and this Sungat be able to believe this? The fortunate girl replied and spoke thus:—"O great king we are residents of Agra, and belong to Khutree caste. My father, who was the prime minister of the Emperor of Dehlie, died. The emperor hearing this, attached all

---

[1] Meant by Brahma, who was first created by God and appointed to create the rest of the world.

[2] Compliments, homage.

[3] Aha! Well-done!

our property and secured it by sealing the padlocks of the store-houses and appointing Police guards to watch over it. After this the emperor asked whether my father had a son and was told that he had seven daughters and that my mother was pregnant with the eighth child. The emperor ordered that the attachment will be removed if the pregnant woman brings forth a son. After sometime a son was born, bands of joy were played and the glad tidings were carried to the emperor, who immediately removed the attachment, drew away the Police guards and fixed daily allowances in the name of the infant. I then told to my seven sisters, Blessed is the man's beard! for the sake of which the whole family is released and by means of which all religious devotions and adorations are accepted and bring forth fruits. Beard is highly esteemed in the presence of God and in the court halls of men. Without the beard and Turban, there can be no distinction between male and female! O true king I am sure that they removed the attachment as soon as one male was born in the family and no one paid regard to the existence of seven females. Blessed is the true beard!! A curse' is pronounced at the birth of females and the words, "Well has it been"! are uttered at the birth of males. Beard is the fruit of divine services, and pleases the seer as much as if he had seen the sacred face of God. A man having no beard is like a Satan and should not be trusted. Hearing this the Gooroo said, Blessed is thy belief O girl! and then addressing the seikhs said, 'O Seikhs. Kase (long hairs worn by Seikhs on head) also are as excellent as beard. It is improper even to look at the face without beard. Here ends the 43rd Sakhee.

' A custom prevailing in India.

SAKHEE FORTY-FOURTH.

Once a certain number of Seikhs, who were in attendance of the Gooroo, said O true king, you can do as you like, but some money is urgently required for necessary expenses and the winter is also drawing near. They were saying this, when a merchant arrived and paying homage to the Gooroo, placed the sum of Rs. 2,000 before him. The Gooroo asked him, whose follower he was and where he lived. The merchant replied that he was a resident of Mooltan and was the follower of Peer[1] of Nagáha, that he had brought a large supply of merchandise, but could not sell it off, that he enquired if there were any true Gooroo[2] or Peer in this country and was told of the addressee's name, and having succeeded in obtaining his object had brought the 10th part of his profits as present before the Gooroo. The Gooroo replied, O Seikh brother, whose field is *his* corn shall be. If a stranger drives away a cow grazing in the field, he does not by this act become the owner of the field. Go and give offerings to the Peer, whose follower you are. The Gooroo does not wish to rob persons in the way. The merchant said, O Gooroo I have only related my past story, but be pleased to believe that since I have received benefit from the Gooroo's house, I have become a Seikh. Please forgive my past sins. Hearing this the Gooroo said O Seikh those who belong to Hindooism are mine, but Mahammedans are my enemies, I have lifted up my sword to kill them. Those who are theirs are not mine and those who are mine are not theirs. O brother to become a Seikh, to wear long hairs on the head, to give alms and to fight are all easy tasks, but it is difficult to remain faithful. Without faith it smells badly and good faith

---

[1] A Mahammedan Saint, whose shrine is Nagaha village about 100 miles west of Mooltan,

[2] The Gooroo is a Hindoo Saint or spiritual guide, and Peer a Mahammedan Saint or spiritual guide.

has a sweet scent, which soothes the brain. Faithless persons get no rest either in this or the next world. Faith guards against all evils and the house of faithless is ruined. No one becomes the spiritual guide of the faithless and such a person is, Baba Nanuk says, unguarded like a fenceless field. The merchant embraced Seikhism at the moment and continued to send heavy presents from time to time. The Gooroo placed full confidence in him and he used to come now and then to the Gooroo with a large Sungat. Here ends the 44th Sakhee.

SAKHEE FORTY-FIFTH.

Once the Gooroo went to Malwa country, the people of Burar nation crowded around him and served him and always carried out his orders. The Gooroo wanted to go out for hunting. Dulla Barar always attended the Gooroo, who therefore first went to his house give "Durshun" to his wife, the daughter of Chumbal in previous birth. (See last part of Sakhee 40th.) After this the Gooroo went off hunting and after killing a deer, laughed. Dulla Burar asked for the reason of laughing and the Gooroo told him, O Dulla! this deer was a Seikh of the Gooroo in his last birth. He had spoiled and stolen much of the treasures of the Gooroo. O Bhai Dulla Barar whoever will embezzle other man's property will have his flesh cut and shall be killed. All the deers and goats are such persons of the last birth as had embezzled their Master's money. I had advised him very much but he did not listen to me. Then looking towards the killed deer laughed and said, did I not forbid you? After this, the house being too far, the Gooroo determined to pass the night under a "Keeker" tree. The Seikhs complained of hunger, saying that they were unable to move. The Gooroo ordered them to go up the Keeker tree and to shake it well. It was done so, and all sorts of sweet-meat such as, "Julebee," "Phenian," "Khoorme" &c., &c., began to drop in showers from the tree. The Seikhs ate it and were satisfied. Some of the Seikhs did not eat this sweet meat, saying that they will not eat unless the Gooroo first eat it. When the eating was over, the Gooroo said, blessed are those who have not eaten, for those who have eaten are only slaves to their belly. Some Seikhs are slaves to their own wishes, O Brother it is very far to become a true Seikh. After this the Gooroo went to his house and taking meals went to his bed and rested. The night became very long. The people and animals were put to much inconvenience. Here ends the 45th Sakhee.

SAKHEE FORTY-SIXTH.

The next morning Dulla said, "This night has been very long! All the villagers confirmed his word and said, yes, it was so. Dulla, then, accompained with the Sungat asked the Gooroo with folded hands of the reasons of this. The Gooroo replied, O Dulla Brother, a misunderstanding had arisen between the sun and other gods, last night. So on one side, the sun declined to do his work and sat silent in a corner, and on the other side Inder[1] was displeased and drew back from his work. Hence there was no rain and the night had become long. Dulla then said "O Gooro, how shall we be saved without rain"! It is long since we have had no rain. All the Sungat also entreated the Gooroo with folded hands for rain. The Gooroo then spoke with anger, "O Bhai Dulla, beat the Inder and believe in my word. Dulla threw up shoes seven times towards the heavens and railed Inder and said, Send rain O worthless! you had obeyed the order, likewise we obey the order. The Gooroo then repeated the verses, which mean, "The sun or moon are afraid of him" &c.,

---

[1] King of Gods and rains.

up to the end. After sometime it began to rain in the Malwa country and there was an abundance of grain and other products of the field. The Gooroo then returned from Malwa and said, " There is much compassion in the Malwa country, but there is good deal of falsehood. It has received nourishment from the money procured by selling daughters in marriage, so there will be plenty of corn but no satefulness. They (people of Malwa) will always be panting for wealth and will change their castes for the sake of bread. The seikhs of this country will go abroad to acquire sovereignty and will become independent Rajahs having no emperor to control over them. Here ends the 46th Sakhee.

SAKHEE FORTY-SEVENTH.

Once the whole country was suffering from the severe attacks of fever, when Dulla with the permission of the Gooroo proclaimed that whoever wants to be saved from the fever should keep Kase (or long hairs) on the head and should read Gooroo's word. Sungat being terrified fled to "Dumduma Sahib and began to read Gooroo's word. All, who did so were cured from the fever. The Gooroo then ordered them to build a " Dhurmsala[1] " and to be engaged in the service of their fellow Seikhs for, he said, by so doing they will in future be saved from fever and will enjoy comfort and rest. The Sungat began to carry out the Gooroo's order and to read Gooroo's words. Those who had gone to live there for the sake of religion and mercy were confirmed in the Seikhism. Here ends the 47th Sakhee.

---

[1] A Religious Institution where strangers are received.

SAKHEE FORTY-EIGHTH.

One day the Gooroo was extremely pleased and said, "O Dulla Burar, ask something from me! I am going to Roper," Dulla bowed his head and asked for rain. The Gooroo was silent for some time and again said, ask something O Burar. The Burar again wanted rain. This was repeated three times and on the 4th occasion the Gooroo said, "No reliance can be placed on Jut's[1] words," Bukkal's[2] silence, Gooroo's orders and Brahman's relationship. "Now prepare for the rain," the Gooroo exclaimed. The rain began to fall in abundance and continued till three days and three nights incessantly. The people were filled with terror and exclaimed, "Save us O king," "Save us O king." Dulla came and bowing before the Gooroo, requested that the rain be stopped. The Gooroo laughed and ordered the rain to be beaten with shoes. It was done so and the rain stopped. Few days after this the Gooroo left the place and was followed by fifty Seikhs. They reached Chumkaur and put up in Nibala Chowdree's[3] house. All the people made Gooroo's Durshun that night, and the Sungat began to crowd around him. Among these there came a Khutranee woman of Machheewara[4] and paying homage to the Gooroo placed a piece of cloth before him. The Gooroo told her to ask for what she wants, and she said she was unable to walk and obtain Gooroo's Durshun and that she used to give presents to the Gooroo from the proceeds of her spinning labour, but now she had grown too weak even to do this. The Gooroo told her that she should take back her cloth for the present, and that shortly afterwards he (the Gooroo) will visit her house and at that occasion will accept the cloth from her and will wear

---

[1] Clown.

[2] Corn-dealer.

[3] A Lumberdar or chief in a village.

[4] A village in the District of Loodhiana.

it. The Gooroo then gave her some Prashad[1] to eat and she ate it. The Gooroo, then, stopped there for few days, but the fair of Sun's eclipse drawing near and a great crowd having assembled at that place he made preparations to go to Koorchetur.[2] Here ends the 48th Sakhee.

SAKHEE FORTY-NINETH.

One day when the Gooroo was at Koorchetur he happened to meet Muddun Nath Jogee,[3] who spoke to him, saying your dress is like lions, but your acts like devotees. The Gooroo said, O Nathjee, the wicked Mahammedans cannot be subjected without punishment. The Jogee then asked him whence he had obtained supernatural powers. The Gooroo replied, "that Baba Nanuk was a perfect saint and it was *he* who granted me these powers. My dress is like worldy men and my works are done by God. My attention is always fixed to do whatever God wishes, whether it be good or bad." The Gooroo and Nath were mutually pleased by this conversation and the latter asked the Gooroo to accept some assistance from him. The Gooroo replied that his both arms being strong he required no assistance from him, and that his army was well up in the art of archery. The Nath then requested the Gooroo to show him his skill in archery and the Gooroo discharged an arrow, which pierced a wall of the Moghuls fort situated at great distance. The Nath was astonished to see this and said, O Gooroo, wonderful is thy art of archery! no one has been so skilled in it, except "Arjun"[4] in "Dwapur[5] yog." It is sure that Mahammedans will be annihilated at your hands. I live in

---

[1] Something, generally sweetmeat. fruits, piece of bread &c. given by a devotee servant of a shrine or temple and any religious man to his followers or laity is called "Prashad."

[2] A famous place of Hindoo pilgrimage near Umballa.

[3] A sect of Hindoo Devotees.

[4] One of the famous heroes of "Mahabharuth."

[5] The 3rd Age according to Hindoo accounts.

Kutas,[1] please come there necessarily to see me ; you will find me in Sidh's[2] residence on "Balgondai" hillock. The Gooroo said, "O Nathjee it is not God's will that I may go there, but my Seikhs will visit that place. It will be 13th century[3] then, and the Mahammedans will be killed. I will leave this body on the banks of "Godaveree" river, where also many of the "Sidhs" live. Saying this they exchanged "prashad"[4] with each other. After this the Gooroo went to see the city and was met with all the Brahmans of Koorchetur in the parlour of "Attun Shah" which was situated on the banks of the sacred Tank, and in which the Gooroo had put up. The Gooroo granted "gold-mohurs," horses and daggers to these Brahmans. One of them named "Kainkree Ramdutt" constantly attended the Gooroo, who told him to ask for something, as there was nothing wanting in the Gooroo's house. The Brahman said, "I want nothing O Gooroo, only do not leave my arm and assist me whenever I need your assistance." The Gooroo, then, said to the Brahman, "I will call you with your family, I have now filled your house." Saying this, the Gooroo caught his arm and took him aside and bought three horses paying off 1,000 Rs. as their price. After this many people came to see the Gooroo, who (next day) early in the morning went alone to "Awul Khairee" station. Three hours after his arrival the Seikhs joined him and in the meantime an old woman recognised the Gooroo and laying hold of the reins of his horse stopped him and said, O king, eat something. The Gooroo said, bring whatever is ready, and the woman brought a large quantity of milk, which was drunk by all the Seikhs, who said, "We have seen great faith in this old woman"! The Gooroo said, a saint will be born from the womb of this woman and she shall also be born in a Zamindar's house,

---

[1] A sacred place of Hindoos in Jhelum District.

[2] A perfect devotee.

[3] According to Mahammedan year.

[4] Ex. B.

and one who shall be born from her womb shall be a Jutee.[1] Oode Singh then asked, "O.Gooroo, where is that person now." The Gooroo after remaining silent for some time said that Futteh Sing will be born from her womb. Oode Sing then asked, O great king, why will thy son be born again. The Gooroo said, "Such is the will of God." Oode Singh said, Sir, please tell me about my futurity also and the Gooroo said, O Oode Singh, you will be the chief of Seikhs for 4 times and the 5th time when the years of the 13th century will pass away, I will turn the seikhs into Tulungas[2] and will destroy the English by a look and the Khalsa, at last, will assist the Rajpoot sons thrice. Here ends the 49th Sakhee.

SAKHEE FIFTIETH.

Once the Gooroo asked water from his servant named Zalum Singh, saying, "O Zalum Singh, I am suffering from severe thirst, please give me a cup of water ! The servant being absent at that time, a seikh boy proud of his great beauty spoke out, O Gooroo Jee, shall I bring the water? Saying this he stood up with great love and bringing a cup of water gave it in the Gooroo's hand. The Gooroo took the cup of water in his hands, but looking at his (boy's) hands, said, O seikh brother your hands are very delicate ! what is your work ? The seikh boy replied, "O Gooroo, I have never worked, nor have I ever served my family and your seikhs. Only I have brought this cup of water for your to day. Hearing this the Gooroo threw away the cup of water, saying, " What a great sin ! I have touched my hand with the hands of this unworthy Seikh ! The seikh was ashamed and fell upon the Gooroo's

---

[1] One who never enjoys sexual pleasures in his lifetime is called a Jutee. Just opposite to lustful.

[2] A man of N. W. Provinces, employed as a soldier in the British army is called a "Tulunga."

feet, Saying O Gooroo, I am your old pupil of Churn Pahool ceremony, and am a literate youth, please forgive me. Upon this the Gooroo said, "a man does not become Seikh by learning, but by faith and service, you have not served any body, how may thy hands be considered holy? The feet also only *then* become holy when we walk with them to Teeruths[1] or to obtain the "Durshun" of sages and devotees. Likewise the whole body is purified by serving and O Brother the water of thy unholy hands is like a dead corpse. Hearing this the young Seikh consented to serve and caused his past sins to be forgiven. From that day he began to serve Brahmans, devotees and travellers zealously and thus earned the pleasure of the Gooroo and the plauses of the whole Sungat.

After repeating this Sakhee, the eyes of the Boodha Sahib were closed by the effect of extreme love and interest in the Gooroo's words. When his eyes were reopened, all the writers were filled with joy and said, "What a good Sakhee has this been related"!

The night approached, and Boodha Sahib said, "O Seikh Brethren, the Gooroo only will forgive us, we will see to-morrow about the inaccuracies and errors of this story. The 50th Sakhee is finished to day in the month of Jaith Sub 1781, Sunday. The remaining 49 Sakhees will be related to-morrow.

---

[1] Places of Hindoo pilgrimage.

HERE ENDS THE FIRST PART.

SECOND PART.

SAKHEE FIFTY-FIRST.

The Boodha Sahib resumed his task and began to relate the remaining part of Gooroo Gobind Singh's biography. He said, that once Budden Singh Khutree of Bairi tribe and resident of Agra came to the Gooroo, in his presence and after compliments said, "O Gooroo, I am come to see you, please tell me about Mahammedans what do you wish now, what is it proper to do?" The Gooroo replied O Dear Seikh, hear from me what will come to pass in the age of "Kuliyoga." I relate it to you, the Seikhs will also be profited by it. There will be a Bunya [1] named Dhurosa in Kulka City, which will be many miles in circumference. A daughter will be born in the house of that man and she shall be a woman devoted to divine worship. She shall remain in Purdah till the age of 20 years after which she shall be seen by a King named Bissul, who will fall in love with her. He will send his servant to her house and will fetch her forcibly to his house. The Mahammedans will be much vexed at this. In the 20th year of the reign of Mown's [2] queen there will be great disturbance caused and every one will be out of order as evil spirits are. The images of stones will be broken and Hindoo temples will be demolished. The rule of the Emperor will be overthrown. There shall be mutual fighting and they shall be destroyed. The Rajahs will be powerful. Battles shall be fought in every house and village: Horses, Elephants, Ruths,[3] and wealth will be plundered. In the year 19th

[1] A corn-chandler.

[2] Englishmen.

[3] A carriage of Indian fashion.

the heroes will rise and Mowns will plunder the streets and villages. The fear will be first felt in the Malwa and then in other countries. The Mahammedans will not be allowed to stay even for a moment. The Seikhs will devour them as the lion devours the animals. The people shall be trembling for 5 years, and will not be able to sit comfortably in houses, temples, streets and paths. After this, O Budden Singh, a religion as good as those of Sutyoga will be spread. There shall be a virtuous King in the town of "Dipdeepun," who shall beat and drive out the Rajahs, and shall issue small coins. O Brother, there are many discrepancies in the said and heard accounts. There is no end of such accounts. The name of that King* will be Ram Singh and the people of mean castes will be afraid of him. He shall make the world alike, that is, one good religion spread throughout the world. He shall keep the officers of the Seikh army with him and by their council will reign and kill all his enemies. He shall not sit long on his throne, but shall die soon after his accession, after this a great dust-storm will come, elephants and horses shall be released and the men will fly. The thieves and rogues will plunder, the sons will be separated from their fathers, and brothers from brothers. The beggers will be found in possession of wealth and the people, of all four Asrums[1] will be put to trouble. The charity and the performance of munificent acts will fall to dust. The people will suffer for seven years in this manner. The 8th year will be better. At that time there shall remain 20 years of the Ganges's age. Hill Rajahs will lose their kingdoms. Mahammedan's forts shall come in the possession of Seikhs. All the virtues, respective ceremonies of four castes and precepts of the "Vedas," which had been forgotten shall be resumed. Mahammedans shall be des-

* The Kookus think this Ramsing to be the same Carpenter's Son.

[1] There are four Asrums according to Hindoos *viz.* one Brahmchurj or school-life, second Ghirust or married-life, third Bansprust or Demi-retired-life, fourth Sumast or total retirement.

troyed and the Khalsa will arise. The Seikhs being collected will fight near Dehlie and dressing themselves in nice clothes will plunder the town of Paniput.[1]

The Khalsa will reign for two hundred and fifty years altogether. One hundred and thirty-five years of this will pass with the perfect tranquility, and seventy-nine years will pass in tumults and disturbances. At that time you, O Budden Singh, will be known to the public as the helper of my Khalsa, your name will be "Teja Singh," and Duleep Singh my Seikh will arise. Here ends the 51st Sakhee.

SAKHEE FIFTY-SECOND.

The Boodha then said, I am going to sing the Gooroo's praise, O Sahib Singh, you write it. I tell you these things according to the Gooroo's orders and have an eager desire for the service of the Gooroo's feet. This Sakhee had been told to me by Goor Bux Singh and not by the Gooroo. The Gooroo had three wives, *viz.*, Mata Jeetoo, the well-wisher of the Khalsa; Mata Sahib Kour, who loved to see the Gooroo's face; Mata Soondree, who had the charge of the Gooroo's food, clothes and wealth. On Sunday the Gooroo went to the house of the first wife and at her request granted her a son named Joojjar Singh. On Thursday the 9th of the lunar month, the Gooroo went to the house of the second wife, and gave her a son named, Zorawur Singh. On Saturday the Gooroo went to the house of the third wife, and granted her a son named Futtah Singh. These three were like the three gods[2] of fire, and were the consumers of the forest-like Mahammedans. Here ends the 52nd Sakhee.

---

[1] A city near Dehlie.

This clause is also interpreted in the following two ways, *viz.*:—1. "The Seikhs will plunder the Railway Train of Englishmen. 2. "The Seikhs will plunder the ocean steamboats."

[2] In the Hindoo Mythology, there are three gods of fire.

SAKHEE FIFTY-THIRD.

The Gooroo went again to the house of his second wife, and granted her another son named Jeet Singh, who was skillful, and acquainted with the art of using weapons. All the four sons were as wise in their childhood as old men, were handsome, well-wishers, and obedient to their parents. The accounts of all the four children are pleasing. The Gooroo showed a great skill of Kok[1] science in enjoying his wives. There is no order to relate the following 3 Sakhees which give detailed accounts of the mutual pleasures derived by the husband (the Gooroo) and wives from conjugal intercourse. The 54th, 55th and 56th Sakhees are therefore omitted.

SAKHEE FIFTY-SEVENTH.

One day a battle was fought between the Gooroo and the Hill Rajahs. All the Seikhs and the mother of the Gooroo held a counsel on that occasion and said to themselves that without executing the treaty of peace they shall be put to much loss and that they should therefore go and advise the Gooroo to make peace with the Hill Rajahs on the ground that they had been fighting for 40 days and that the enemy was assisted by the Khawaja, a Military Officer of the Mahammedan Emperor, who had undertaken to obtain victory for the Hill Rajahs, and had therefore marched with great army for the purpose of defeating the Khalsa, who had been surrounded on one side by the Hill Rajahs and on the other side by the Mahammedans and that there were only 40 Seikhs really faithful to the Gooroo and that other men and the Gooroo's relations considered the Gooroo as mad. Having considered this, the Khalsa accompanied by the mother went to the

---

[1] A science of enjoying women, prescribing rules, methods and medicines by which conjugal pleasures may be best obtained.

Gooroo and said O Gooroo, now the only way of safety for us, is to apply for peace, please agree to what we propose. Hearing this the Gooroo said, Hill people are all worshippers of stone and their brains are consequently dull like stones. They are liars, perjurers and 'false-looking fellows.' Saying this the Gooroo ordered his treasures to be loaden on bullocks and bound the treasurer by oath of the cow, "Shiva" and "Thakoor" not to give out the secret, that rubbish was laden on the bullocks. The treasurer by the order of the Gooroo loaded 5,000 bullocks and sent them out in the night. The robber Hill Rajahs seized the bullocks and drove them to their camp and were extremely pleased. When they opened the loads of the booty they found nothing but rubbish. They felt much grief and sorrow at this, and said they had been repeatedly deceived. The Gooroo then said to the Khalsa, have ye seen the second fraud ? On the other side the Hill Rajahs punished their men, who had plundered the bullocks, and sent vakeels to Khalsa to settle the terms of peace. The Khalsa accepted it and came to the Gooroo with these vakeels, who having paid fines[1] and presents to the Gooroo explained all the secrecies of their heart. The Gooroo said I do not err, but I have consented to what my mother and the Khalsa say. They executed the treaty of peace which was signed by the Khalsa except the 40 Seikhs, who were truly faithful to the Gooroo. Here ends the 57th Sakhee.

SAKHEE FIFTY-EIGHTH.

The Gooroo then accompanied by his two wives set out for Malwa and took 40 Seikhs with him. The rest of the camp followed after and had reached near the Ghunowla[2] village when they were attacked by the Moghuls.

[1] For the crime of plundering bullocks.

[2] In the district of Amballa.

Both armies fought with bravery and many of them were killed. The Gooroo, who was skilful in arms heard this, stopped and saw that the Mahammedan army had besieged the Seikh army and the heroes of both side were fighting. Seeing this the Gooroo lifted up his arms and opposed the enemy. At that time all military Seikhs with folded hands begged the Gooroo to go out from amongst them as there was no hope of their being saved. The Gooroo hearing this request repeated several times, understood that such was the will of God, and then made over all his military dress worn at that time to one Oode Singh who exactly resembled the Gooroo in features. Oode Singh wore that dress and by the order of the Gooroo began to fight. The enemies took him for the Gooroo and opposed him. Oode Singh pushed them off as the Indra had done with the demons. The soldiers of the Gooroo also fought in the battle of Ghunowla and after a long and steady fighting were killed. Many of the Seikh heroes were fighting even after their heads were cut off. The forces of the Mahammedans and Hill Rajahs made horrible oppression and the Seikhs fought and gave their lives for the sake of the Gooroo. The Mahammadens then killed Oode Singh, under the impression that he was the Gooroo and after killing him thought that they had killed the Gooroo and were pleased not knowing that they were deceived and that only Oode Singh was realy killed. The Gooroo had silently escaped from that battle as the "Krishn," had escaped from the Hill, which was set on fire by "Jarascinde." After the death of Oode Singh the Mahammedans hearing that the Gooroo was still alive, proceeded to search for him and ran as the night runs after the sun beams and can not catch them. They plundered the Seikh camp near Rooper, but the Gooroo fled and hid himself in the Forests. The rest of the Khalsa took refuge in the houses of Mahammedans, who fearing God, mercifully abstained from killing them. The Gooroo's wives went to live in the house of a Dilliwal,[1] who was also a Seikh of the Gooroo, and no one knew of this fact. On the next morning the Gooroo arrived in Chumkour, as Raja Ram Chand leaving his family had gone to live in forests. The Gooroo was separated in the night from the 40 Seikhs and no one knew of what God had ordained. In the Chumkour the Gooroo fought with 10,000 Mahammedans, the Chief of which named Khawaja, wanted to seize the Gooroo fraudulently. The people were enraged to learn this and prayed to God for the annihilation of the Mahammedan's power. The Seikhs entreated the Gooroo to leave the battle, saying that if *his* life will be saved, the root of the Seikh religion will remain firm, and thousands of Seikhs like them will be created. The Seikhs repeated this supplication several times in the night and the Gooroo, laughing, discharged an arrow, which killed 10,000 enemies at once. The Gooroo by so doing made every one believe that he was all powerful, but it being the age of Kuliyoga he does not like to have his supernatural abilities known to the world. After this the Gooroo complying with their request escaped with the two Seikhs. The Kali[2] clapped her hands behind the Gooroo and said, behold! Hindoo's prophet is flying! Seize them who assist the Seikhs. When the storm of the great tumult arose, the Gooroo fled to the Southern country and on that day he was obliged to travel on foot for 15 miles. He then halted at Machheewara, where the Toorks followed him beating their drums and besieged him in the night. The Gooroo then called "Ghunee Khan" and Nubbee Khan "Puthans" and asked them for a place, where he could pass the noon-time. He then put on the blue clothes and gave out himself as a Hajee.[3] The Ma-

---

[1] A Resident of Delhie.

[2] A goddess in Hindoo mythology, to whom human sacrifices are made.

[3] A Mahammedan pilgrim of Mecca.

hammedans being suspicious of fraud gave him rice of Niaz[1] to eat, which the accompanying Seikhs avoided under the pretence that the Hajee was in the habit of keeping fasts since one year. Ghunee Khan and Nubbee Khan Puthans ate together with the Seikhs, who, passed the knife through the food and repeated the words "Tav Prashad" (Thy kindness). The food turned into "Karah Prashad." Having seen this, both the Puthan brothers believed the Gooroo to be a true Saint. The Gooroo when he went out of the village at the time of departure, granted a letter to the Puthans, the contents of which were that all the Seikhs of the Gooroo should pay whatever they can as present to these Puthans whenever they produce that paper.* The Gooroo then said to the Puthans, "I have given you the reward of my service." Here ends the 58th Sakhee.

SAKHEE FIFTY-NINTH.

The Gooroo was once walking on foot in a state of complete absorption in divine love and was accompanied by two other Seikhs when a third Seikh came and fell upon his feet and recognizing the Gooroo gave him a horse to ride upon. The Gooroo accepted the horse and ordered the accompanying Seikhs to go to their respective houses. The following events happened in the absence of the Gooroo from his family. Mata Goojree, the Gooroo's mother, and two sons of the Gooroo died. It is difficult to relate this painful story. The Mahammedans of Sirhind had killed the Gooroo's sons and had buried them under a wall. Hearing this the mother fell down from the place and expired, as was the case with Devki[2] in the separa-

---

[1] *i. e.* rice dedicated to Mahammedan prophets or sages.

* And the Patta which the Gooroo gave to the Puthans is known to all as an order or what we may say, *hookoomnama* and the very Puthans showing the order or *hookoomnama* to the Seikh Rajahs, take certain amount of money as reward at every half year.

[2] Krishn's mother.

tion of Krishn. The Boodha Sahib says, that the sinful rogues killed the poor children. The firm roots of Mahammedans were extirpated. O brother, hear the unexplainable story of the Gooroo. Nothing was known of the Gooroo for three months. One Sumeer, resident of the Kanger [1] village heard of the Gooroo's arrival and went to the place where the Gooroo was put up. He fell upon the feet of the Gooroo and said, you are my spiritual guide, please accompany me to my house. The Gooroo laughed and said I am the enemy of Mahammedans and you are subjects of the Mahammedan Emperor, it is not safe for you to take me to your house. He agreed to meet the danger that may befall him, and took the Gooroo to his house. This man Sumeer* was a heroe of his promise. The Gooroo after arriving in Kanger was engaged in hunting, killing hogs and riding on horses, &c., &c. The Gooroo remained there hidden like sun in the clouds. Sumeer, the great, always waited upon the Gooroo, who was pleased and ordered him to ask for anything he wants. He begged that he wished to be emanicipated from the pain of undergoing 84,00,000 sorts of birth. One day the Gooroo gave him the leavings of his meal and sad that the pains of births will be annihilated. He took the leavings to his house and distributed them to his relations. They were afraid to see the flesh of a slain hog and chided Sumeer, saying that the Peers and Googa [2] ruin the people. They returned the Prashad to Sumeer, who went next morning to the Gooroo, and being asked of what had passed, he related the whole story before the Gooroo and fell upon his feet saying "Save me O Gooroo." The Gooroo ordered him to come the next morning. When it was night the Sumeer fell asleep and like "Soo-

---

[1] In the district of Ferozepoor.

* This Sumeer is a Dhaliwal Jat and a resident of Kanger, and his own descendents live in the Mouza Dina.

[2] A Peer worshipped by both Hindoo and Mahammedans, who was born with a serpent shadowing over his head.

khdev[1] Sowamee" in a dream saw himself transmigrating into the body of a swan, crow, animal, parrot, insect, man, woman and again man. He found himself born hundred times in the "Malwa" country and being once hungry ate some Peeloo[2] fruits and felt thirsty. In the mean time he was awakened and found a chewed Peeloo fruit entangled in his teeth. Being astonished he went and said to the Gooroo, O lord! you only know your things! The Gooroo replied, O my Seikh you have undergone all the births and now, therefore, stand emancipated from further trouble. The Sumeer fell upon the Gooroo's feet and said he has been very fortunate on account of the Gooroo's hiding himself in his house. I am saved by the Gooroo's stay in my house. After one year the well-behaved Gooroo went to "Dumduma Sahib" and lived there for 3 years minus some months and days. In the mean time Aurungzeb died. The Gooroo read the news of his death and understood the whole story. Here ends the 59th Sakhee.

SAKHEE SIXTIETH.

By the Gooroo's favor, Khalsa's desire was completely obtained, viz., Bahadur Shah ascended the Delhie throne and Aurungzeb expired.

The reigning Emperor began to search for a saint and called the Gooroo with great humility and supplications. The Gooroo heard his message and promised to see the Emperor on his way to the Dukkun.[3] Shortly afterwards the Emperor heard of the Gooroo's intentions to start for Dukkun. He went on foot to receive the Gooroo on the way and brought him in Delhie. The Gooroo lived in Delhie for five months and accomplished three different

[1] An ancient sage of Hindoos.

[2] The name of a wild fruit.

[3] The Southern part of India.

works in that city. The Gooroo's pupils begged the Gooroo to send for his wives. The Gooroo denied and advised them to serve and to take care of his wives. The Gooroo then dismissed the accompanying Seikhs and told them that they and the two wives of the Gooroo should not see the Gooroo again. The Gooroo further told them that he was much pleased with them. After this the Gooroo built the tomb of his father "Tegh Bahadur" at Delhie and made friendship with the Emperor. The Gooroo then expressed his intention of going to Dukkun and the Emperor treating him with great kindness begged him to stay more for some time. The Gooroo said, that he was anxious to see the Sacred River of Godávari and that he (the Emperor) should be looking after his two wives. The Emperor then dismissed the Gooroo with great respect and returning to his house highly served and took care of the Gooroo's wives. Boodha Sahib said, O Brother, I was not with the Gooroo at that time and therefore I am not an eye-witness to the above said facts which I have only heard from some Seikhs. O Bhai Sahib Singh, I tell you the truth that Mata [1] Sahib had taken me with her with the order of the Gooroo, who also blessed me saying that my faith in the Gooroo will be permanent and strong. O Brother, when I left the Gooroo, he went to Dukkun and felt thirsty in the way, the water was searched for and a Seikh brought a cup of water and said to the Gooroo that he had brought it from a Brahmani's house who lived very purely. The Gooroo hearing this, threw off the water and said it was not pure as it was brought from a single woman's house. The house in which there are many children is holy. O Brother, it is the faith and not outward washings which make the man pure. The water of the house in which there are many persons, is always pure and therefore the house of family-man is holy. Even "Devtas" do not eat in the house where there is a

[1] Meaning mother, here meant by Gooroo's wife.

single man, such a house is cursed. O Brother, a devotee whose mind and body is pure is better off while alone, but the house in which there are many persons is holy. The body, mind and wealth of such persons are all pure. After this the Gooroo arrived on "Pohkar Teeruth" and gave alms to his "Prohit"[1] "Chetun" on the same Ghat,[2] where "Baba Nanuk" was complimented by "Sidds." The Prohit asked about the caste of the Gooroo and was answered that he (the Gooroo) was of the 3rd caste "Khalsa." The people were astonished to hear this and considered the Gooroo either a saint, a nobleman, or a prince. On the other side of the Tank there was a shed in which there lived a Thug[3] but was known by the ignorant public as a devotee. He used to kill travellers from off by an arrow. All the people told of the wickedness of that person to the Gooroo, who replied that there shall come a good Seikh to kill him. After this a "Moghul" named "Mokkubber Begh," a resident of Delhie came to see the Gooroo, whom he attended for 3 months and accompanied to the sacred rivers Ganges and Godáveri. The Gooroo at the time of departure granted him a sword 10 Seers in weight. On proceeding further, a young man servant of the Mahammedan Emperor met the Gooroo like a lion. After this the Gooroo observed *that place* on that banks of the Godáveri, where he had passed his days in worship in previous births. When the Gooroo wanted to occupy that place, a number of quarrelsome "Moghuls" prevented him from doing so. The case went before Shah Bahadur, who decided it in the Gooroo's favor. The Gooroo showed the signs of his former worship at that place.

The Emperor granted four square miles of land to

---

[1] A family priest.

[2] A ferry. A place on the banks of a river or Tank.

[3] Robber.

the Gooroo. In this land the garden[1] of a Bairagee[2] was situated. That Bairagee belonged to "Ram Kuman" sect and was habituated to sit on a large couch every day and to eat the food baked by himself. The Gooroo, as engaged in hunting-sport reached that garden and killed a deer belonging to that Bairagee and ate it. After this the Gooroo went and stood before his door. He was engaged in offering food to idols and a sheet of cloth was hung before the idol hall to hide it from public view. The Gooroo without any hesitation went and sat on the couch with the military dress that he was wearing round his body. The followers of the Bairagee prohibited the Gooroo from sitting there and the Bairagee himself was enraged. The couch from the weight of the Gooroo's body began to sink in the ground. The Gooroo said, O couch, what enmity have you with me that you are flying away from me and are sinking down in the ground. The Bairagee in the meantime seeing that the couch was stopped from sinking downwards fell upon the Gooroo's feet and said O true Gooroo, forgive, and do not regard my actions, I will do whatever you order, your word is full of kindness. Hearing this, the Gooroo said I want to spread my religion and will kill Mahammedans, by the order of Gooroo, O devotee, what do you think it well to do, speak the truth, I ask thee. The devotee replied, O Great King you are the Master and I am your servant, I will not hesitate to carry out your orders. Hearing this the Gooroo said, I have picked you up as the gold from sand, go in the Punjab to substitute me in killing my enemies. I have granted you the superintendence of my followers. Saying this, the Gooroo began to grant Jouhurdar[3] weapons. The Seikhs seeing this filled their eyes with tears and began to weep and the hairs over their body became strength. They asked

---

[1] A garden of Indian fashion, i. e. a fortified garden with buildings and Halls in it.

[2] A sect of Hindoo devotees.

[3] Marked with blackish beautiful marks as well tempered steel.

the Gooroo to grant the bow to the Bairagee but not the sword. The Seikhs further said, "we have taken protection of thy feet, do not reject us. Hearing this the Gooroo said, O brothers, I give these for my own work and by means of this the descendents of Khalsa will enjoy pleasures. After this the Bairagee said, "How will I be able to manage this business alone, I can act with your assistance." The Gooroo, hearing this, said, in your army and cooking room there shall be thousands and lakhs of Akalees.[1] Saying this the Gooroo asked the Bairagee to shut his eyes. He did so and when he opened his eyes again, he saw some Akálees in the sky. Seeing this Bairagee fell upon the Gooroo's feet and said, O Gooroo direct me what to do. The Gooroo said O brother, protect the Seikhs of the Gooroo and kill the wicked Mahammedans and you should keep yourself pure and meet the Khalsa with Pahool ceremony. If you will please the Khalsa, you will obtain your desire. When we will occupy all the territory we shall possess greater glory than any one else. Saying this the Gooroo became silent and gave two good seikhs to Bunda Bairagee as his personal guards. The Gooroo showed good way to those Seikhs i. e. gave them permission to plunder the cities and streets and to feed themselves by these means. Sakhee 60th finished.

SAKHEE SIXTY-FIRST.

The Bunda then took leave of the Gooroo and was created the General of the Seikh army which amounted to 8 lakhs and 7 thousands ready men. The Emperor of Delhie was filled with awe at that time. The Bunda then defeated and pursued the Mahammedan's army and after this plundered the following countries turn by turn, viz., Jungle Koorchetur, Poadh, Sundhora of Mahamme-

---

[1] A Seikh fanatic.

dans, vicinities of hills, Surhund which was reduced to ashes. Then they proceeded quickly and plundered all the-cities situated on Sutlej Banks. They plundered Loodhiana, Magha, and southern countries. The distressed people wanted to protect their property. After this he plundered Goordasspoor and the people fled. Baba Boodha or Goor Bux says, that we also arrived in the mean time. All the Seikhs told us that the Gooroo had adopted that Bairagee and had granted the superintendence of Seikhs to him. The Bunda Bairagee then came to Amritsur and here his attention was drawn to the ceremonies of Bairagees and he wanted Khalsa to adopt those ceremonies. The Khalsa being unwilling to do so adopted the opposite ceremonies i. e. began to wear blue clothes and to drink wine. The Bairagee wanted to have *his* ceremonies observed and the Khalsa wanted to follow their own way. This complaint of the Khalsa reached the Gooroo in the Dukkun. All wore the uniform dress and exclaimed before the Gooroo who ordered Khalsa to go to Amritsur and called the Bairgagee in his presence, but he (Bairagee) refused to go. The Bairagee knowing that all the Seikhs had rebelled against him, fled to the other side of River Scinde in the night, taking with him such persons as had remained faithful to him. A merchant informed the Mahammedans that the Bairagee had fled with the Gooroo's treasures and the Gooroo has taken away the miraculous power from him. Hearing this the Mahammedans took the treasure from him by force and the Bunda Bairagee was killed in battle. After this a Seikh, the grandson of Futteh Singh hid himself in the hills and the Khalsa having received arms was awakened by the Gooroo's favor. Boodha Sahib said, in my presence, the Khalsa attacked the Mahammedan army who fled and lost their glory. The grandson of Futteh Singh named Nund Singh began to roar and the following persons, who paid regard to Seikhism joined him, *viz.*, Deva Singh,

Attar Singh the hero, Mudden Singh and Ram Singh the faithful, Kuppoor Singh, Goor Bux Singh, Chota Singh and Sujjun Singh. These men remained engaged fighting and killing for a long time. After this Nadur Shah marched against the Moghuls of Delhie, who were overawed. Nadur Shah emptied the whole world and O brother I saw no master of the India at that time. I have seen this with mine own eyes and I believed all the words of the Gooroo to be true. O Seikhs, hear with pure and attentive heart what the Gooroo has said:—Once the Gooroo had predicted to me certain things and I sat silently and disinterestedly near the Gooroo. I questioned about the futurity and the Gooroo answered as follows:—"In the Kuliyoga the people will lose their faith." The Gooroo on being asked by other Seikhs said, the Seikhs will first conquer the country of Punjab, after which they will conquer Jhelum, the "Bist Doab," the Cis-Sutlej territories, the Malwa, the Koorchetur, and the territories bordering on hills. In the Sub 1860 the followers of Christ will conquer the east and the Seikhs at the same time will plunder the "Khadur" country. After this the Seikhs will conquer the country between Ganges and Jumna Rivers and the Delhie territory. In the mean time a person will be appointed to reign in the city of Delhie. They will then join and attack my followers, who will consequently be made to suffer and will repent and will say to themselves, "what will the God do now," while the Seikhs will be in such thoughts the Sub 1897 will approach and after that in the Sub 1899 disorder will prevail in the countries and then a king will arise and protect these and will root out the other Rajahs. All the people will fall in difficulty and my Sungat will become obedient to the Christians, who becoming displeased with my Seikhs will dismiss them and send them away to their houses. After this the power of one God will be felt on all four sides, the warriors will remain towards the west and trans-Attock territories. After this one Hindoo protector named "Moola," a Seikh of the Gooroo will fight and conquer the countries. Sakhee 61st finished.

SAKHEE SIXTY-SECOND

When the Gooroo resided in the "Hasegurh"[1] town, he once being filled with love and pleasure ordered that Nund Lall will answer the questions that the Khalsa wishes to ask from the Gooroo. Hearing this order Nund Lall collected all the copyists. He was in the habit of calling the royal sects and copyists in the presence of the Gooroo, in order to please him (the Gooroo). The Gooroo at that time had been angry since one year. When the Gooroo had worn long hairs and had established the Pahool ceremony at that time, the Seikhs of all the four castes had turned away from the Gooroo and used to say among themselves, "The Gooroo has become mad, he has caused the Brahminical thread to be thrown away and shrubs[2] to be worn on the head." Once the Gooroo gave, iron, seeds of sesamum, oil and Manh[3] in alms and ordered his Ardasia to distribute these to good Brahmans. Each of these things were hundred maunds in weight. The Ardasia said, O true king the Brahmans do not take it. The Gooroo said, "what do the Brahmans say?" The Ardasia said, O true king you know yourself, saying this, the Ardasia felt afraid and the Sahib Singh, who was sitting by, said, O true king, the Brahmans say that the Gooroo has broken his caste, for he being a Khutree has put off the Brahminical thread and your brethren of the "Sodhoo" family also say that the Gooroo has become mad. Hearing this the Gooroo ordered, spears, rings, bangles and rosaries, to be made of iron. The Gooroo's order was carri-

---

[1] Now called "Anundpoor Makhowal" in the district of Hoshyarpoor.

[2] Long hairs.

[3] A kind of grain in India which is boiled and eaten with the bread.

ed out and these things having been prepared out of the iron given in charity were brought before the Gooroo by Sham Singh in the evening. The Gooroo then repeated the following verses which mean :—" O God you yourself are the giver and the enjoyer of all things, thou givest and thou doest, thou art the creator of all things, thou givest the life and retaketh it, saying this the Gooroo distributed two chukkers,[1] a chain, and five spears to each of the seikhs, who took these with pleasure. The Gooroo then said, Khalsa is the Gooroo's shape and the Gooroo is Kalsa's shape. Khalsa will be the proector of the poor and refugees and the resting place for those who have no house. Brahmans are entitled to receive alms but they have now left the Gooroo and the Gooroo has left them. The Gooroo further cursed the several sorts of Brahmans and said, the Gooroo will become like pieces of Bricks and " Sanoubries" like the mat and the " Kankoobja" like stone. The Seikhs will push them away like rubbish. The " Prohit" seeing the Gooroo enraged, stood with folded hands. The Gooroo then said to the Prohit, the " Sarsoot" will remain with the Khalsa, who will consider you holy beggars no matter in whatever dress you remain, your descendents will spread and will live in " Sumbhulpoor" and your family will be known by the name " Bishanjus," and will protect the people. In this family the Nihkulunk Awtar[2] will flourish who will save the people from calamities. After this Sadhus[3] folded their hands before the Gooroo, who said, " I am the superintendent of Seikh religion, whoever likes me as a Gooroo, his family will be increased and he will be worshipped like myself. My Seikhs should adopt to live in my town. The Khutrees were then afraid and with folded hands fell upon the Gooroo's feet. The Gooroo said, "if you will be subject to my

[1] Iron circles worn by the Seikhs on head around the knot of hairs.

[2] Incarnation of Deity.

[3] A well known family in India to which Gooroo Gobind Singh belonged, here means the persons of that family.

religion, I will consider you as my Seikhs. The Khalsa has collected taxes from all the world." The Gooroo then granted the following things, viz. nobility the prime-ministership, devotion, policy, ability of protecting wisdom, generosity, arts of bows and guns, political abilities to Oode Singh, Mohur Singh, Dhunna Singh, Dan Singh, Man Singh, and Churt Sing, Zemindars and then went away to his palace, where his wife Mata Jeeto, fell upon his feet and said, "O great King, what will your sons do, you have granted the chiefdom to other Seikhs." The Gooroo laughed and replied, "you be lords of the true house and then all will obey you and your family will enjoy eternal chiefdom. Saying this the Gooroo closed his eyes and immerged in religious contemplations. The Mata Jeeto, then bowed herself before the Gooroo and went away, consenting to what the Gooroo said. Sakhee 62nd finished.

SAKHEE SIXTY-THIRD.

Baba Boodha then said, "O Seikhs whatever is the Gooroo's will, shall come to pass in the future."

Once the Gooroo was sitting in a Durbar and was surrounded by Beer Singh, Aspal, Mudden Sing Rajpoot and several other Rajahs. One Sham Singh asked the Gooroo at that time, O true King, Khalsa is little and his enemies, Hindoos and Mahamedans amount to a great number, how will then Khalsa be able to reign. The Gooroo replied, whoever will be liberal in eating and other expenses, will be dear to me, I will please those, who will go to fight. My Khalsa will bring all the wealth of the oceans. I will take them to paradise, who will be steady in battle. The Khalsa will arise, who they will fight both hungry and satiated and will consider the battle as the sacred war of "Mahabharuth," such a person notwithstanding his being engaged in the worldly pleasures, will obtain that high celestial dignity, which devotees obtain by religious austerities. The Khalsa will also obtain the true knowledge and the power of divine contemplations. In the Sub 1930, 1949 and 1950, the Khalsa having become master of the world, will be diminished. After this the Khalsa will reign over all the countries between Khadur,[1] and the ocean. No Rajah of the Seikhs will be able to establish himself on the throne of Delhie. Gooroo Nanuk is able to forgive! such an age will come that new women will break the heads of those who have shaved hairs. In the Kaliyoga this war will be like "Mahabharuth" war and the wicked will be destroyed at this time. In this Kuliyoga "Pandavas" will reign for 1000 years. Anund Rajah will reign for 1,500 years, and after this Souruj, Mouruj, Toorj, Moghul and Puthans will reign for 4500 years. Again Khalsa will reign for 50,000 years. After this there will be no king for 575 years. No regard shall be paid to friendship. A king will then arise in the Dukkun and northern countries[2] and will be governed by Europeans. When Duleep Singh[3] will arise, there shall be no comfort left for the Rajahs. A way shall be opened through Malwa, "Koorchetŭr," Jungle, Majha, Attuck, Kashmeer, Hansee and Mulikpoor. The Peshawer, Jullalabad, and Kabool will come in the possession of Seikhs. The Khalsa then will hide himself in Scind and will wear new dress to conquer the Dehlie. The Gooroo then said, O brother, that[4] person will be of my shape and complexion. Duleep Singh shall be born as incarnated. Aurungzeb and his essence shall be absorbed in my essence. I will embrace him in arms in the house. He will enjoy the sovereignty of Lahore and Kashmeer for some days and will afterwards reduce the Khalsa to subjection. I will assist him, and the Gooroo will be of

[1] Jeend teritories.
[2] Or Lahore territories.
[3] Deep Singh of.....................
[4] Referring to Duleep Singh.

Khalsa and Khalsa will be of Gooroo. Hearing this the Seikhs bowed down and asked, "shall we be able to obtain the Gooroo's Durshun. The Gooroo said, I will be present in the Khalsa. Sakhee 63rd finished.

SAKHEE SIXTY-FOURTH.

The Gooroo after giving the above stated account of the futurity was silent. The seikhs further begged him to reveal the future things in detail, and said O Gooroo, your followers are anxious to know about their success or failure in the future. The Gooroo replied as follows :—

The age of Kuliyoga is 4,32,000 years, in which a devotee of good actions can get rid of the troubles of several yogas. I have heard the secret things explained by the "Bias" in "Bhivishut Puran." I will explain to you those as mingled with the things revealed to my mind. To this I will also add some of the things spoken of by Baba Nanuk. Out of the whole age of Kuliyoga 2 lakhs of years will pass away in the virtuous discharge of duties of 4 castes, one lakh will pass in the faithful discharge of the duties of 4 "Asrums," fifty thousand will pass in sensual pleasures, twenty-five thousand will pass in sins, two thousand will pass in boyhood, two thousand will pass in foolishness, ten thousand will pass in visitations, five thousand will pass in "dust-storms" and the remaining thirty-eight thousand will pass in the rest of the worldly enjoyments, making the total four lakhs and thirty-two thousand years. In this age "Kulgee" "Awtar" will flourish, the speeches of false disguisers will be taken as truth. If any person wishes to see the image of Kuliyoga, he should go out of the city for one year every day. He will then see the Kuliyoga in the shape of a fat man, totally naked, eating a piece of bread in his hands, wearing blue clothes, speaking and laughing.

Seeing such a person, a man should bow before him and address him saying, O great king, my sins are destroyed by seeing you, and my bodily superstitions are removed. Whatever the Kuliyoga will speak upon this, will be found true upon deep consideration. The Kanvun will reign for 10,000 years in Mugdh[1] Desh in the beginning of Kuliyoga. After this "Kanvun" will kill the prime minister of the Mugdh Desh and will take up the reins of the Kingdom in their own hands. Fifteen hundred years after this, Nund Raja will reign and will reduce all people to Shooder caste by force like the "Purs Ram." After this the race of a king from the womb of a Shooder woman will reign till five generations for five hundred years in Souruj,[2] country. For five hundred years after this Sourjee will reign. For three hundred and fifty years after this Mourjee will reign. For seven hundred years after this Toars will reign. After this Moghuls will reign for one hundred years. After this Puthans will reign for 12 years. After this again Moghuls will reign for 375 years. After this Toorks will reign for 575 years. When 4,025 years of the Kuliyoga age will pass the following events shall come to pass, viz., a Moghul named "Mahi" will flourish and will reign for five hundred years. After this the origin of the Seikhs will spring up, and Mahammedans will be vexed by them day by day. The Toorks will remain as long as the "Ganges." In the meantime the English worshippers of the sun will reign. After this the king of Nepal will reign. The Seikhs will then root him out. After this when the 1800 years of the Hindee Sub will pass the seikh's power will increase. In the year 1819 a season of plenty will ensue and in the year 1818 a famine will happen. In the year 1907 the English power will be established, after having been sprung up in the year 1902. After this a great famine will come and

[1] North western Provinces.

[2] Country South East to "Meruth."

the Rajahs will be destroyed. After this those Englishmen who will go astray shall be removed. In the year 1900 every house will be dreary. At that time the Seikhs will follow the ways of Khalsa. After this Oode Singh * the incarnation of the Gooroo will flourish and Duleep Singh will be lighted like a lamp. He will crush the Hindoo Rajahs in the Jummoo Deep. At this time one house will be ruined and in the other songs will be sung. In some house worship will be made and some houses will be decorated. Some will become like dead. Three hundred years after this Maleches,[1] will reign and no wise man will be discovered up to the shores of the sea. Thus 1000 years will pass. after this the Maleches will prevail and their ceremonies will be observed. The women will become powerful and the Rajahs weak. Then a great disorder and tumult of the Kuliyoga will be caused. When 38,000 years of the Kuliyoga will remain to pass, the Vishnoo will appear in "Kulgi Awtar." I will come that day mounted on a horse back. We shall kill and be killed. We shall be dissolved in heaps of ice as high as man's stature. All the Khalsa will then throw off their bodies and shall obtain the dignity of martyrs. After this the Khalsa being purified shall joyfully go to God's regions. This will be the end of Khalsa. All this will pass over them like a dream. The Goor Bux Singh also called Ram Kour, who belongs to Ram Das's family reciting the above said words of the Gooroo became silent and falling in the sleep of sacred love secretly enjoyed the pleasures of salvation. The Kuliyoga will become a slave of the person, who will read, hear or write this future history of Kuliyoga. The sins of such a person will fly and love of God will be produced in his heart. Sakhee 64th finished.

---

* This Oodee Sing was called by some people Bhai Oodee Sing of Kainthul.

[1] Nations against Hindooism.

SAKHEE SIXTY-FIFTH.

Once when the Gooroo was sitting in contemplations he said, O my seikh in Kuliyoga age you should believe in me only, I become incarnated in every yoga to do good to my followers. That seikh who behaves according to my admonitions is the crown of my head. Hearing this the seikhs asked with love, saying " tell us O Gooroo what are thy admonitions, how should we live and how should we treat others. The Gooroo replied, O Khalsa, whoever will be converted to seikhism by " Kase Pauhul" ceremony, will obtain salvation. The Pauhul is of two sorts, (1) Sword Pauhul, which is celebrated by stirring the sweet water with Sword, (2) Churn Pauhul, which is celebrated by drinking water with which the feet of the Gooroo are washed. Whoever wears Kase without Pauhul ceremony is a fool and shall not be able to see my face; such a man should be driven from the community. It is always good to remain in one religion, for no one can live in two. Whoever, being called my seikh, subjects himself to superstition is a sinner. There are 3 sorts of seikhism, viz. (1) Sahjee, (2) Kurnee, and (3) Khund. A seikh who wears Kase, completes all the 3 kinds of seikhism. These my Kase wearing seikhs are of 3 sorts, (1) Sookeshee, (2) Oopkeshee (3) Bekeshee, who are also called " Moonduts." My seikh should strictly observe the ordained ceremonies and should bathe at 3 o'clock in the morning. He should read Goormookhee and should give up joking. He should obey Gooroo's order like Veda's words and should shun the precepts of other religions like illness. He should not read Persian and Arabic characters. He should not bow before a Mahammedan, no matter he serves any body. He should not eat while sitting near a Mahammedan. He should not covet friend's wealth. He should not make friendship with mountaineers. He should treat with the people of four castes as follows :—

Whoever being a Brahman is a simple seikh or a seikh of Churn pauhul ceremony, he should leave others. It is not good to give charity to a nominal Brahman. Covetous Brahman should be rejected, and should not be seen by my seikh. A Sooltanee Brahman should be abandoned. A Brahman, whose forehead be undaubed with wet sandal powder, should not be looked at. Whoever will give charity to such a Brahman, as is in the habit of backbiting the seikhs, shall die. A Seikh of Sword-pauhul ceremony should not give Pind,[1] to his ancestors for it will become sand. If he wants to give any thing to his ancestors, he should give dresses, wealth &c. to his seikh brothers. A Brahman who is not my seikh should not be provided with food even. A similar treatment should be made with the Brahman, who being a seikh of Churn Pauhul ceremony makes himself known as that of sword pauhul ceremony. A Brahman who is converted to seikhism by Pauhul ceremony, but does not wear Kase, should be forsaken. A Brahman who wears Kase just for the sake of plundering my seikhs and gives up the rites of ancient sages, shall be like Kate.[2] Brahman is better than three castes and is the appearance of three gods. If he changes his religion or worships the Mahammedan Demi-prophets, he deserves the punishment of being thrown into the well. That Brahman, who wears Kase is like the old Hindoo sages and one who takes Churn-Pauhul is half better than the former. We should not give even water to that Brahman, who though he wears Kase, is a pupil of some other Gooroo or worships petty gods. A person should serve my seikhs and not give water to such a Brahman as above said. A Brahman who wears Kase for the sake of livelihood is like a Chun-

---

[1] An oblation to deceased ancestors as a ball or lump of meat or rice mixed with milk &c.

[2] The mythological name of the descending node, represented as a headless demon.

dal,[1] and charity given to such a Brahman is wasted. A person who being in seikh religion, worships Seetla,[2] and gives charity to a disguised Brahman or eats the Prashad, of all sorts of shrines, should never be considered as my seikh. I will forsake him, who shall worship gods without asking me previously. My seikh should feed the poor when he goes to a Teeruth or when he wants to give charity on sacred days, he should give either to those who believe in the Gooroo or to those who are attached to Gooroo's institutions. My seikh should not look for Teeruth Brahmans, when he goes to Teeruth, for they disguise themselves and make a great show. A seikh should live alone and should not entangle himself in the love of others. He should always be thinking of me and should feed seikhs. One who does not wear Kase is like poison to me. A Brahman who sits in the company of virtuous seikhs though he does not wear the Kase, is like Bias,[3] to me, and my seikhs should give charity to such a Brahman. A seikh should give his daughter in marriage to a seikh only and should not take the price of daughter from her husband. Such a seikh of mine will go to my regions. My seikh should not worship Seetla, Peer,[4] Sooltan,[5] Yogee,[6] and evil spirits, but should worship the Gooroo only, such a man will go to Durbar. A seikh should always read Anund,[7] and Jupjee,[8] whether little or more. He should also hear Rouhrass,[9] Artee,[10] Showla,[11] and religious songs. When a seikh and his wife sit together, they should teach Gooroo's songs to their children, such as the following verse, viz. "Remember God always over and over again." When a seikh of Khutree and Bunya caste may wish to prepare

---

[1] A professional sinner of mean appearance.

[2] A famous goddess of Hindoos said to be lord of dead and grave-yards.

[3] A well known Hindoo sage, the author of Poorans &c. &c.

[4] and [5] Mahammedan Demi-prophets.

[6] A Hindoo devotee of the "Gorukh Nath" sect.

[7] and [8] Sacred Treatise in the Grunth or Holy Book of Seikhs.

[9] [10] and [11] Sacred songs and praises in Punjabi language composed by the Gooroo.

food for the sake of making offerings to the deceased ancestors, he should call a seikh Brahman only to prepare such food. A seikh should not give those kinds of mean charities, which are given with a view of throwing one's own evil upon another, who receives that charity; for the receiver of such charities goes to hell. A seikh should only confine his prospects to the Gooroo and should not pant after the pleasures of this or next world. He should always bathe and engage himself in contemplations. If a seikh does not observe these ceremonies he will be subject to sorrow and mournings. I have no relation with those seikhs, who are adulterers and who read Persian for the sake of earning their livelihood. A Seikh should not drink water from the house of a seikh who reads Persian, nor eat any thing from his hands, nor trust him, for he has relinquished the way of faith. That Brahman, who being my seikh, will maintain himself by marriage or Saradh[1] fees, will be a great sinner, for he deprives the poor of their right. That Brahman, who sells the offerings made to planets or sells his knowledge or the sacred verses of " Gayitree" or sells the charity given to him at the time of the eclipses of the sun or moon, goes to hell. My seikh should bathe, worship, make sacrifices to fire, and give water to the deceased ancestors at the time of eclipse. When the eclipse is over, my seikh should give Charity and be thankful. A Brahman who takes Charity at the time of eclipse, is guilty of the offence of suicide. My seikh should throw such a Brahman into a deep well. That Brahman who belongs to a good family but being in reduced circumstances receives mean charity, is like a Malech and cannot go to heaven. My seikh should keep aloof from such a Brahman, who sells his daughter in marriage, takes charity at the time of eclipse, eats offerings made to gods. Such a Seikh will go to my regions. Whoever being a reader of my

---

[1] Ceremony of giving food to the deceased ancestors.

Grunth appropriates the presents made by the Seikhs or sells the books &c. copied by himself, is not my follower but, a false backbiter. One, who does not take alms and does not pay regard to Hindoos and Mahammedans is my real and true Khalsa. One who does not touch the limbs of a "mean-charity taking Brahman," is mine. I will live with him. My Seikhs should earn their livelihood by means of arms, for such is the custom of Khutrees. It is good to give alms to a contented Brahman, for he will thereby maintain himself and remember God. I do not love castes and outward dresses, but faith and strict observance of my precepts. The true Gooroo has related this routine of Seikhs' life with great attention and love; whoever will read or hear it, will obtain sweet enjoyments in this world, and after his death will go to the Gooroo's regions. Sakhee 65th finished.

SAKHEE SIXTY-SIXTH.

Once the Gooroo was sitting in a peculiar state of mind and a Pundit was reading the history of Mahabharuth. When the account of Pandavas[1] was recited and finished, a person spoke out saying, "no one has ever risen from the dead, what do we know what happens in the next world ! whether any thing after this happens or not."

At that time Nund Lall spoke, "Our acts are bad, but there shall be a good end of those who have faith in the Gooroo."

Again *Sainaput* said, the Gooroo's " Durshun" saves a man, whether his actions be good or bad, the true Gooroo mends them.

Again *Oode Rai* said, we reap according to what we have sown, as the seed is so shall the tree be.

---

[1] E. B.

Again *Ramul Kubhee*[1] said, the essence of our souls, which is similar to the spirit of God, is free from good and evil, and we entangle ourselves in covetousness according to our own will. Again *Alloo* said, this body is senseless and five elements disperse. Our intellect and breath are even lifeless, that which is living within us is nothing but God himself, whatever ye all say is truth, the divine spirit neither kills nor is killed. No other person is like him. As fire is only like fire, coldness is like coldness, purified butter, is like purified butter and water is like water, so, if we destroy the outward delusion, we find no other but God. Again *Chund* poet said, that the connection between God and the human soul is similar to that between the moon and the partridge and between the mother and her son.

Again *Bolloo* Baishnav[2] said, unless man hears (the religious books) he does not understand the similarity of God and the man's soul. Again *Sukha* Poet said, "whoever bears 1,00,000 maunds of weight, he shall be pressed under it and those who have no weight upon them will laugh, likewise is the case with virtuous and sinful man.

Again *Eshur Dass* said, this world has no real existence in any of the three tenses and whatever appears is nonentity. There is no doubt in this.

Again *Sookubeea* said, "as a man in a dream can form thousand sorts of shapes, so by divine contemplations the forgotten truth is re-sprung.

Again *Dhurm Singh* said, " It is very good to remain in one's own religion, and to worship the god he has hitherto been worshipping. This matter is supported by the Veda." Again *Dhian Singh* said, "to keep one's

---

[1] Poet.

[2] Follower of Bishnoo.

self aside from the wordly pleasures is the cause of leaving the world altogether and to contemplate upon the feet of the true Gooroo is the best wealth."

Again *Mala Singh* said, "we should be acquainted with the repetition of the name of the true Gooroo. There is no other business which can impart four sorts of blessings, viz., Dhurm[1], Arth, Kam, Mokh, better than this."

Hearing this discource, the Gooroo said, To keep one's self aloof and to look on the rest of the world with an eye of equality (i. e. to be equally honest and kind to all the creatures whether mean or honorable) is the best practise of Yoga science. Three castes are entitled to read Vedas, viz., Brahman, Khutree and Bais, the fourth, the Sooder, is not authorized to read them or to learn the sacred principals of salvation. One who is always thinking upon the question, " who am I and what is this world"? will know himself and will obtain salvation. One who wishes to enjoy worldly pleasures let him do so according to Vedas and at the same time abstain from heinous crimes. If any one has a very great desire for carnal enjoyments, let him indulge in them after hearing and fully understanding the Vedas. One who cannot leave the sensual pleasures, is lazy to do good acts and does not worship the gods, but for the sake of obtaining success in worldly undertakings, is a fool and soweth seed in the dust. That person who has an eager desire to be saved, has been acquainted with the pains of births and deaths, and has known himself through the true knowledge of the Vedas, is joined with the Gooroo. As the man's inclination is, so shall the desires spring up from his heart. We should recognize that Holy spirit from which we derive rest and comfort. One who has acquired perfection from a perfect Gooroo, shall never lose. What is poor salvation before the dignity

[1] All 4 before explained.

obtained from such a Gooroo. When the five sorts of breath, viz. Pran, Opan, Saman, Byan and Audian are separated, the foolish men call it death. These five sorts of airs rejoin; as in a dream man sees whatever be had been thinking of when awaking. There is no better cause of salvation than to annihilate one's desires to reduce his mind to a state of calmness and to immerge himself in divine thought. Other ways of salvation, viz. complete subjection of the mind, complete subjection of the senses, abstaining from carnal pleasures, practices of yoga science, giving public feasts, Religious austerities, charity &c. are useless without good company, as the menses of a barren woman. All sorts of worship and religious ceremonies are initial steps of finding God just as all the marriage ceremonies, viz. forming a pompous marriage procession, calling a wise Brahman for the purpose of worshiping gods and binding particoloured thread round the right wrist of the Bride and Bridegroom, making all the women sing marriage songs, are initials to the pleasures of being joined as a happy pair. One who does not recognize such a God, what shall his end be! Blessed is the birth, family, city, knowledge, arts and skill in poetry of that man, who has fully understood the essence of his soul and cutting off all his relations with the world has found the one true God existing everywhere. Such theological questions were always discussed in Gooroo's Durbar. That Seikh who will hear this with great attention and will act upon it, shall be emancipated from the terrors of the world. Sakhee 66th finished.

SAKHEE SIXTY-SEVENTH.

Once the Gooroo in order to try the Brahmans gave public feast. He invited Brahmans and told them that whoever will eat flesh, will get one gold Mohur and whoever will eat Kheer[1] mixed with sugar will get one Rupee only. When the Brahmans had done with the eating the Gooroo acted contrary to what he had said, viz. he gave one Mohur to those who had eaten Kheer mixed with sugar, and one Rupee to those who had eaten flesh. The Gooroo afterwards explained why he had done so, saying that those Brahmans who have eaten flesh were covetous and those who have abstained from eating flesh were good Brahmans. The Gooroo further said, hear O Seikhs one who eats flesh is not a Brahman. All the Sungat heard this and asked, O Gooroo what is your order for that Brahman who has been converted to Seikhism. The Gooroo said, O Alum Singh, my good son, a Brahman by adopting the military duties of a Khutree has ascended the throne of Indra. His Brahmanhood consisted in the Khutreeism. A Seikh Brahman should adopt the use of sword and should neither take alms nor go to eat in another man's house. Whoever gives alms to such a Brahman falls in trouble. It is for this reason that I have ordered the Brahmanical thread to be thrown off. It is the pride of a Brahman to abstain from eating and drinking flesh and wine. A Brahman should not kill living being and should not eat flesh ; one who acts against, it is like a Chundal. That Brahman who is void of covetousness, treats every one equally well and remains engaged in talking on theological subjects, is a "Dev[2] Rishee," My order is unbreakable. That Brahman who being a man of family lives in forests, reads Vedas and earns his livelihood by gleaning, is a king of all Brahmans *i. e.*, is best of all. That Brahman who lives in the city, but is virtuous and abstains from envy and backbiting, is a true Brahman. That Brahman who uses arms is like a Khutree, one who keeps a shop, is like a Bunya and one who lives

---

[1] Milk and rice boiled together.

[2] Holy sage of gods.

as a day laborer is like a Shooder. * That Brahman who makes no distinction between eatable and uneatable things, and does not shrink back from wine, flesh and woman other than that legally married with him, is like a Chundal. My seikh should forsake such a Brahman. That Brahman who himself takes the alms but murmurs at other's taking it, is like a cat. To such a Brahman charity should not be given. That Brahman, who takes fees for his acting in the marriage ceremonies or for making worship on behalf of others, is a professional Brahman and is house of sins. One who gives charity to such a Brahman is a village of sins. That Brahman who learns sanskrit, remembers God, gives up praising and backbiting and performs all his duties, is worthy of being praised and of receiving charity. A Brahman should marry only one wife, for Brahmans are not allowed to marry more than one wife. A Brahman should not take fees for his acting in marriage ceremony and should not worship other Gods. He should wear Brahmnical thread according to Veda ceremony and should read Vedas regularly. He should take alms according to the rules of Vedas and should treat all with equal kindness. He should not receive food in alms and should not accept mean and bad alms. One who worships such a Brahman is fortunate. A Brahman should not receive the following kinds of alms.

1. Given at time of eclipse.

2. Grain and other things given by weighing one's own body with them.

3. The vessel full of purified butter in which one has seen the shadow of his own face.

He should keep himself off from the house in which a death or birth may have occurred. He should read "Vedas" or "Poorans" without a wish of obtaining world-

* Here a verse is omitted in the original.

ly things thereby. He, who enjoys what God has given him, is a Brahman of good understanding and is higher than all the world. I have obtained my glory have and acquired the knowledge of true God from worshiping the feet of such a Brahman, I have been able to establish my religion through the favors of such Brahmans. I am not born for nothing. My seikh should not take charity nor go to eat the charity food in another man's house. My seikh should live desireless and pass the days of his life with thankfulness. He should maintain firm the faith taught to him by his "Gooroo." He should seek the way of improving his faith and should do his works and make enjoyments at their proper time. He should give up foolishness and read the words of Gooroo. He should not be selfish and serve every body whether he be good or bad. He should not keep the company of mean fellows. One who breaks his promise all his works are false. Whoever is called my seikh, should take "Pauhul" and be virtuous. When he comes to the Gooroo his past sins forsake him. He should not worship demons, evil spirits, and stones. It is the custom of Kuliyoga to worship stones. The advantage of worshiping graves, and, "dead-burning grounds," is false. One who shuts his nose and makes use of his rosary for the sake of show, is highly impure. That person in whose mind the love of God is not produced wanders about to "Teeruths." The stream of Ganges water and the sacred songs of God are equal. One who remembers God is saved. Sakhee 67th finished.

SAKHEE SIXTY-EIGHTH.

The Gooroo *said*, O seikh brothers, one Deep[1] Singh will be born and will make the false persons straight. My Seikhs will be everlasting, their actions are shining. In the Kuliyoga, whoever out of my Seikhs will be virtuous

[1] Deep Singh of.................................

will be saved, all is useless without faith. O Seikhs once my followers had fought in the battle of Bhungani and had enjoyed rest in Anundpoor Makhowal. When the battle was fought at "Nidown" mountaineers fled. At that time Moghul army arrived from Lahore. All the Hill Rajahs deserted each other and killed the chief of Mahammedans. The God saved me at that time and killed my enemies. All the battles were complete at "Lukhnowtee" village. The army of the king of Delhie attacked and many of them were killed. The Khalsa. fought many battles and conquered many. We destroyed all and obtained victory. We bost our heads for the sake of religion. The Muleches are now even too numerous, the Seikh heroes will kill them all. Believe these my instructions to be true O patients, do not forget. My Seikhs will increase and every house will have his own king. After this one of my Seikhs will fight for the sake of religion and will conquer Kussoor. He will be glorious and Master of his own senses. After this battle will be fought there shall be war among the Rajahs in each house. When many years will pass there shall be a king in the house of those Seikhs, who shall be highly glorious and will assume the form of Khalsa. After many days the Khalsa rule will be established. He will conquer, first, the mountaineers and then the Kashmeer country. There shall be a mountaineer Seikh whom the Khalsa will treat with treachery. That Khalsa killing each other among themselves will be annihilated, as a heep of hail is melted in an instant. The "Diamond"[1] will be destroyed and the "Lamp"[2] will shine. No Seikh should try to explain this enigma, if any one knows it, he should keep silence within himself. The Boodha Sahib then said that the kings meant in the above, stated enig-

---

[1] Meaning Heera Singh son of Dhian Singh; the prime minister of Seikh Government.

[2] Meaning Maharajah Daleep Singh.

ma will be Seikhs, saying this the Gooroo's attention was drawn to examine arms. Four Ghurees after this the Gooroo said, O Alum Singh, * thou art a great "Rungheer"![1] Alum Singh said, O Gooroo I am your Seikh. The true Gooroo said, O brother, the iron cuts iron and the Rungheer kills Rungheer. Behold, I have put the Rajahs under your subjection; you shall be born in the house of Rungheer, I give you half Seikhism and the whole kingdom. Alum Singh said, "will I be able to see you in that birth? Gooroo replied I have also a desire of visiting Ramsur in Amritsur. I shall reside there to guard my field, the Khalsa, 11th time. No one will be able to know me and the rule of Khalsa will spread widely at that time. The holy men will be annihilated at that time and the Khalsa will suffer and will remember me always. I will be reborn on that day when there shall be plenty of Seikhs. The foolish, impatient and hidden Rajahs will be annihilated in the wars. All the houses of "Sirhund" city will be demolished and my family will be ruined. As Krishn of "Yadav" family had destroyed his family, I will similarly cut my family like grass. There shall arise five Seikh chiefs. I tell this as an enigma, no one should ask me to explain this. I bind you not to do so by my son's oath, saying this the Gooroo stood and went to see the horses, after which he was pleased and enumerated them. Then he went to cooking-room and took his meals, and fed his Sungat. After this the Gooroo went to his bed and the Sungat departed to their respective houses. Sakhee 68th finished.

SAKHEE SIXTY-NINTH.

The Boodha Sahib further said O Seikhs, to remember and to repeat the name of the true Gooroo, is the best

* And this Alum Singh in the opinion of many others, is said to have taken his next birth amongst the Rungheer cast and the leader of the Rungheers in Raicoot.

[1] An obstinate and stubborn nation in India, proverbial for their obstinacy and blind bravery.

gain. One day a Seikh woman came to the Gooroo and began to weep. The Gooroo asked her the reason of weeping. The Seikh woman said, O true king, my husband had started from his house to obtain your "Durshun," but was killed in the way. What shall I do now! I live in Jullalabad. I have suffered much in this foreign country. Hearing this the Gooroo ordered the Sungat to wear arms always. The Seikhs carried out the Gooroo's order and understood that arms are the friends of the Sungat. After this the Gooroo hearing of and seeing the fighting Seikhs said, O Brother, you should always read "Bar[1] Bhugotee," which has the effect of destroying Mahammedans. Saying this the Gooroo began to praise those Seikhs, who were brave and anxious to fight in battles. The Sungat were excited against the Mahammedans. The Gooroo's advice was that whoever kills a man taking revenge of his relatives death, he goes to heaven.[2] Hearing this the people were much excited to fight and believed firmly in the Gooroo's words. At that time Seikhs became great friends and loving to each other and began to kill indiscriminately. In some places rejoicings and in some mournings were made. The people then began to be called by their appointed names and to express their faiths. Plenty food began to be prepared in the Gooroo's cooking room and the people used to quench their hunger and to increase in spirit. The Gooroo began to distribute the leaves of "Sal" Tree and said that it will heal the largest wounds. The Gooroo further said, that in past ages one named King Alexander had come to Punjab and had established an institution to teach the science of the different regions and of heavens and earths. He was of 50 years of age at that time: After this he began to live in the north side of "Luduk Nagur" and

[1] A treatise composed by Gooroo Gobind Singh in the Punjabi language on the subject of Devi's war with the demons.

[2] Jihad.

passed 87 years there. He had met me at "Rewalsur" in those days. One year before his death he taught, me his sciences. Sakhee 69th finished.

SAKHEE SEVENTIETH.

Once the Sungat addressed the Gooroo saying, O true king, there are two classes of people, one worship the images and others worship God by contemplations, which of these two is the best? The Gooroo replied O Seikh brothers, all depends upon the heart, to speak truth is the sign of divine love. The image is merely a copy and not the original. We should believe in our past actions. The divine contemplation annihilates the fears of the Judge of the deceased and this is the reason why the devotees engage themselves in contemplations. Consider that man saved whose desires are extinguished, such a man is holy and cold. One who fixes his attention on image, that fool should not be trusted. That Seikh of mine is most human whose attention is fixed on the true God, who is highly engrossed in God's name, whose speech is mild, whose disposition is fair, who knows " Shasters," is an hero and merciful. No one is like such a man. There are three sorts of devotees (1) who remembers the Name, (2) who is engaged on contemplations and (3) who worships stones. One who worships the Name is called God's lover, one who contemplates obtains the pleasures of true knowledge. One who worships stones is called "Tamsee" i. e. demon-like. Out of these three our own way is the first one i. e. worshipping God's name. To read Rohrass and to be engaged in . contemplations is the way followed by Baba Nanuk. The Gooroo has adopted this way in the Kuliyoga. The greatest virtue is worshipping God's name, through which many have been saved. This method is full of virtue. The seikhs have adopted it. I have come to establish peace and to crush Mahammedans. O brother, understand this fully. We wear "Kase" and the Toorks are head-shaved; we wear Kutch,[1] and the Toorks wear pantaloons after their own special fashions. The Mahammedans kill cows. We should hate and give up the society of such sinners. One who eats pig's flesh is the Khalsa and one who kills pigs is the seikh. That seikh of the Gooroo is worthy of attention who supports seikhism. Famine, utmost cold, loving women and self-praise are bad. It is also bad to keep deposit, to be in debt to be engrossed in much love. A man should not give out his secrets to every one. In this manner we should live in the world. We should not seek for ominous moments and should not be constant friends of Physicians nor put ourselves under the treatment of a Physician who is our enemy. We should not learn much of Astrology. We should not ask of evil stars. We should not consult with cowards and women, for by their council man loses success. It is bad to begin any work without consulting, but a secret must not be unfolded. That person who is not covetous is happy with little. We should not make our mind, dream, and wealth known to others. In the morning we should use water and in the cold season bask the fire. One who is hungry should eat bread. The vegetables cooked in one's own house are as delicious as water of life. We should not fall in love with the following things, if they belong to a stranger, and are not our own property, viz. arms, horses, women, house and wealth. The best charity is to give away the following things, viz, land, cow, gold, horses, women, house and knowledge. But to give corn is even better than these, and to read God's name is better than all learnings. Man is the best of all creatures.' O man of good understanding it is said by the old sages, that cloud is the sources of all hopes, Khutree is the protector of all, as woman is the keeper of house, heaven is the friend of all. The

[1] Breeches or drawers reaching to the knee.

birth and death are useless with good actions, Khutree is useless without arms, Brahman is useless without learning and arms wearing Brahman is bad. That seikh of mine who is a Brahman is bad. The learned Bunya is worse than all. That Kutree and seikh who has learned Veda is bad. The Shooder who reads Vedas, the Sunyasee[1] who is married and faithless cannot be trusted. It is bad to be busy in Munter[2] and Tunter[3] practices. We should guard ourselves from the following things, viz :—

(1.) A woman who worships departed spirits.

(2.) A bad boy, and.

(3.) A hero father.

We should not eat too much nor make much use of the intoxicating drugs. My seikh should believe in these things and behave accordingly. Sakhee 70th finished.

SAKHEE SEVENTY-FIRST.

Once the Gooroo went to his palace, when his wife "Jeeto" begged and bowed before him repeatedly. The Gooroo said, O my family person, what do you wish? tell me! Hearing this the wife humbly said, O Sir, are we not human beings? why dont we receive holy instructions? Is it because we are females? you are my Gooroo teach me something about God, I am anxious for this. The Gooroo said mind is the cause of all virtues, and the divine knowledge is obtained by converting the mind. From fixing the mind love is produced. A person should close the mouth weighing his breath and driving his attention inward and apply himself closely to holy songs. A

---

1 A caste of Fakeers in India.

2 Incantations.

3 The science of performing curious acts by means of medicines, such as mentioned in "Boy's amusement."

person doing this enjoys the rest of mind. He should fix his his eyes, sound, and ears to the sacred songs. Thus the mind being retired from all carnal pleasures obtains the divine peace o f mind. He should shut his tongue in the palate and look attentively towards the end of his nose. Doing this he will become dear to the Gooroo. When the breath is confined in the navel attention becomes fixed in the end. A man should confine his attention this way for three months, in the forth month he becomes able to see his essence and to recognize himself. This is the secret way of Yogees. A man should give up desires as a fish moves about disinterestedly in the water. By such a practise mind is won. There are five elements, viz., earth, water, fire, air and sky. From these body is formed. The smelling, tasting, seeing, touching and hearing are called delicate senses and are the root of good and bad actions. There are five sorts of breaths, viz., Pran, Apan, Sman, Byan and Oodan, and the places of these five are breast, feet, heart, joints and veins. Besides these there are other five sorts of airs, viz., Nag, Kutehup, Krikla, Devdut and Dhununjai. These airs are the cause of tears, sneaze, eructations and gapes, and live in the brain of the dead. After distingushing all these, a man should seperate the mind and what remains after this is the living soul. This is the true knowledge, the true Yoga and the true practice of a devotee and this is the Public feast, charity, pilgrimage and hard worship. A man should thus engage his mind in the Yoga practise either in the day or in the night. Before a man begins to exercise yoga practice, he should be in the habit of eating little, after this he should excercise to take his breath towards the brain and shut his eyes. Thus he obtains the view of a beautiful image i. e. God. In this world the comforts derived from body, wealth, women, sons &c. &c. are deceiving illusions, and the world itself is an illusion. By yoga practices a man can find out the true essence, which is the principal thing with the yogees. Saying this the Gooroo granted divine love and yoga science to his wife, who applied herself to yoga and after one year through the yoga abilities left her body. This fame of Mai Jeeto spread out in the world. Boodha Sahib said, "once the Parsram Bairagee had asked a similar question, in my presence, from the Gooroo, who then fully explained the practices of yoga science to him and he was able to obtain salvation by this means. When I asked the Gooroo for myself, he laughed and ordered me to enjoy the excellent pleasures and that we will obtain his Durshun in the end as his feet are in our heart from the very beginning." Boodha Sahib further said, O Sahib Singh, this Sakhee has been granted to me by the Gooroo himself, you write it for the Seikhs. This imparts Salvation. Sakhee 71st finished.

SAKHEE SEVENTY-TWO.

Once the Gooroo addressed his Sungat saying, Well worthy of praise are women, divine songs, and Kuliyoga the king of all yogas, for the Kuliyoga[1] has saved many sinners, the divine songs has saved monkeys and the women are extremely merciful. In this Kuliyoga there is no necessity of reading six Shasters, for the person who has fixed his heart in the holy name of God.

There was a fowler of Jheewer caste who one day kills many birds after which he killed sparrows. The birds began to mourn and cry horribly. The fowler then contemplated in his heart that many devotees are engaged in worship in this forest in which he has killed so many birds and many Rajahs leave their royal pleasures and engage themselves in the forest. What a sinner I am that I have killed birds in such a forest. O I have com-

[1] i. e. God has saved many sinners in the age of *Kuliyoga*.

mitted a great sin. Let us go to Bikramjeet Emperor, the Great Generous. Thinking this he set out and met the Emperor who was coming with his army from the opposite side. The Emperor arrested the fowler and imprisoned him for five days. One of the female slaves of the Emperor was moved with compassion and disguising herself like the fowler, put herself in the confinement and allowed him to escape. A month after this the Emperor ordered the fowler to be produced, and the female slave, the daughter of Bunya that was brought before him. She had bribed the guard not to reveal her secret to the Emperor. The Emperor asked her whether she was a man or woman and she replied, O sinner I am the guilty fowler, having eaten the food of your sinner's house, I am turned into a woman. Turn me again to a man otherwise I will kill myself. Hearing this the Emperor sunk in deep thought and said to her that she need not kill herself, he would remedy her. In the next morning the king went out to forest and saw the same fowler, who was sitting there engaged in devotions. The Emperor complimented him but he made no answer. The Emperor then brought the devotee[1] to his house with great respect and made over the empire to him, advising his counsellors to obey him till his return as he was his (the Emperor's) Gooroo, saying this the Emperor departed to forest and engaged himself in devotions. After this the fowler devotee ordered the counsellors to make that female slave sit on the throne and went away himself to forest for devotions. The counsellors then asked the female slave to reign and she said that they should first seize Bishnoo. The counsellors then began to search Bisnoo, the duties of Empire totally neglected and the city became desolate. The counsellors as they were going about in search found an old sage in a mountain cave. They expressed their want before him. The sage hearing all their account knew that they will die in the pursuit if

[1] The fowler who had now become the devotee.

they would not find the Bishnoo. He therefore accompanied them and took them to Jugraj sage on the "Girnar" Hill, and explained all the matter before him. The Jugraj said their king will be turned into a man. The counsellors said, O lord, he wishes to see the Bishnoo.

Hearing this sages brought Bikramjeet and the female slave, whom they turned into a man. Thus Bikramjeet was able to turn the woman into a man and was prevailed upon by the sages to resume the Empire. On that occasion Goruck Nath, Machhunder Nath and other sages came and turning the female slave into a man, made her a counsellor of the Emperor. The sages further said, that *man's body* is the Bishnoo Thus the fruit of mercy was immediately obtained i. e. that female-slave was turned into a man. O Seikh brothers, it was on account of the Kuliyoga that the fowler by a little devotion, became the Emperor's Gooroo and his sins were forgiven. The Emperor behaved generously and the result of this was that he obtained sage's "Durshun." All these persons went to the regions of Bishnoo. Well worthy of praise in the Kuliyoga, the best of the three yogas, for in this yoga man obtaining much reward by little devotion, and it grants salvation easily. Sakhee 72nd finished.

SAKHEE SEVENTY-THIRD.

Once in summer days, large Sungat came to see the Gooroo and were much pleased. There was a great crowd and the Gooroo granted every one their desired objects. At this time a Mudaree[1] beggar rushed in the crowd and reached the Gooroo with some flowers in his hands. He was naked and had become almost senseless by the trouble he had taken in rushing through the crowd and sweat

[1] A caste of Mahammedan beggar.

flowed all over his body. He presented those flowers to the Gooroo who told him, O servant of God, why have you put your body in so much trouble and have brought these flowers? your Durshun was a sufficient present. When you see all with equal eyes, then what is the necessity of presents. The beggar replied that old saying is, "Empty hands have darkened face," "filled hands are rich," "the words of Be-Peer[1] are fruitless," and "the king who has no prime minister, is infidel and empty bodied." Hearing this the Gooroo said, no soul is happy without God's name; the God is the source of all independence, his words are the salvation of the world, one who is devoted to divine worship is acceptable. The beggar heard this and was pleased and said, "Blessed is this day that I have obtained your "Durshun" like Mecca. God's shape is beautiful, I have seen that today. O true king, before I had placed myself at your feet, I went to bathe in a river. When I dived in the water some one got hold of me and took me afar off. I considered this as a dream. I saw a woman in whose body insects were crawling. She took me to a house and treated me respectfully giving me some presents. I saw a man at that time around whose body serpents were wrapped. He called me saying O Sain,[2] I told him that I do not recognize him. He told me, "Go to the 10th Gooroo and tell him that my 1st wife keeps a deposit for him amounting to 5,55,00,000 Rs. and he had sent me 10,70,00,000 Rs. in his last birth, through my second wife, so I possess 16,25,00,000 Rs. for him as deposit, he may take this with interest in each or territory worth so much. He may take it whenever he pleases. Hearing this the Gooroo laughed and said, very good O Sain. The beggar said, explain this secret to me also O Gooroo. The Gooroo said that man was incarnated ocean, the river Sutlej and

---

1 Having no spiritual guide.

2 A name of respect by which Mahammedans or Fukeers are called.

Godáveri were his two wives, I will take account from him and cause this treasure to be given to my Seikh sons. When they will become worthy of reigning, I will take this through a Rajpoot's son. The account is heavy, I will settle this with him. My son and his mother will settle it. For this reason I have told very well, very well, twice, O Sain this is the truth. The beggar said, what will be my condition? The Gooroo said, I will appear in an unknown[1] shape, at that time you[2] will also enjoy the fruits of your labours. The beggar said, save me from the terrors of the world, the worldly enjoyments are diseases and the truth is right. The Gooroo said, O Sain, the proper course is to weigh according to the masters' will. Such is the will of God. All are under His order, no one can act against it. The woman is below and the man above her, I have seen this with my own eyes. The beggar was pleased to hear this and went away. Sakhee 73rd finished.

SAKHEE SEVENTY-FOURTH.

Once when the Gooroo was in Ohumkour all the seikhs of Kabool and Khundar assembled around him and with folded hands asked something from him. The Gooroo said, stop! I will give you something and will cause you to be killed. Hearing this all the seikhs were afraid and kept quiet. After sometime the Seikhs said, O Gooroo give us order to do something and be pleased to allow us to live in the world. The Gooroo said O brother the cloud thunders but the field sparrow-hawk do not care for water, Sandal wood has useful effects, but is of no use until one tree be benefited by it. The

---

1 Ranjeet Singh or Maharaja.

2 Fakeer Ageeguddeena.

River Ganges can wash away the sins, but what can it do if the foolish man will not bathe in it. What can the poor Gooroo do if the seikhs is entangled elsewhere ; sweetmeat is given to the child, but he still eats the dust. A pitcher and rope is in the hands of the owner, why does not well give water ? How can parents relieve their son, if he does not tell them from what he is suffering ; if the sand-wall is giving way, there is no fault of one who white washes it ; if there is no water-pot, how can water be kept in the house ; if a rich man does not enjoy his wealth, but keeps it under the ground, it is no fault of the money ; furnace will not keep hot, if the fuel is not supplied. All the seikhs are engaged in their family affairs. What will the carpenter do if the timber is not sufficient ; how can the water be drunk if the banks of river are not proper and well formed ; how can the food be cooked, if there is no fire in the house ; the wisdom cannot be acquired without time, why should we then insist. The heart is a potter's wheel, from which many earthen vessels are formed. It is so easy to speak out from the mouth, why then should we not advise our heart. The Gooroo gives when the sungat first ask from him. The good or bad actions smite on the face. I will repeatedly sacrifice myself for the person who remembers death. O seikh brothers, I had told you "stop" by which I meant that you should stop your hearts or be contented in your hearts. I had further said, that "I will give you wealth and cause you to be killed," and by this I meant that I will grant you the wealth of salvation and will annihilate the bands of your births and deaths. You wanted to do your household business, well ! it does not matter, there is no haste if the worldy desires still fasten in your bosoms, you better amuse yourself with sacred songs, I have granted you the love of God's songs ; your faith will save you. Be careful ! I will not cross the Sutlej River, all my seikhs should continue to bathe in the

Amritsur Tank. When Gooroo's city (Amritsur) will measure 48 miles in circumference, then O my friends I will come there, and sit upon a throne, and a Chour[1] will be moved over my head.

All seikhs will be collected to the number of five lakhs with horses and elephants and will obtain my "Durshun." My dear seikhs will love plunder, and wealth will be collected in their houses. Join all the sungat no one will be faulty. First Oóde Singh * will come and then the victory will be obtained. A man should commit himself to the God's will as long as he lives. Sakhee 74th finished.

SAKHEE SEVENTY-FIFTH.

Once, the Gooroo had celebrated the Saradh[2] ceremony and had consequently given a great feast to Pundits and all sorts of Brahmans, giving also one gold Mohur to each in cash. In addition to this the Gooroo had given a bed, a cow, a horse, ornaments of men and women &c., &c. On this occasion Pundit Anunt Ram said that the things thus given for the deceased, do not reach them. The Gooroo caused the question to be discussed among the learned Pundits and the truth to be searched out. The Gooroo asked questions without the least prejudice, and the Pundits told him, O Gooroojee, Saradh should be performed at noon time and an invitation to the Brahmans should be sent the preceding night, but the following Brahmans should not be invited to be fed at a Saradh feast, viz.

---

[1] A bunch of white hairs of the tail of a Hill-cow moved over the heads of Indian kings as an emblem of royalty.

* The same Bhai Ooder Singh Raja of Kanthal.

[2] Ex. before.

1 One-eye.

2 Lame.

3 Without legs.

4 One who takes bad kinds of charities viz. a vessel filled with purified butter in which a man has seen the shadow of his face. Images of gold, silver &c., grain, gold, silver, salt, purified butter &c, &c., against which a man is weighed.

5 One who eats in a house unclean on account of a birth or death.

6 The lover of women other than those lawfully married to him.

7 A Thief.

8 A Cheater.

9 A Carrier.

10 The Prime Minister.

11 A Weigher.

12 A Physician.

13 An Astronomer.

14 A Banker.

15 One who takes alms given at the time of eclipses.

16 One who takes horses and elephants given in charity.

17 One who takes a cow given by a man in his last moments.

18 One not wearing Brahminical thread.

19 One not discharging the duty of divine service.

20 Unclean.

21 One who eats bread in every one's house.

22 One who has married many wives.

23 One who takes marriage-fees.

24 One who makes worship on behalf of another man and in lieu of this service takes money from him.

25 A false disguiser.

26 One who does not perform Saradh ceremony himself.

27 One having no wife.

28 A libertine.

29 A devotee of Sunyasee caste or totally retired.

30 "Brahm Gianee" or one well versed in divine knowledge.

31 An illiterate Brahman and all persons of other castes.

32 A Brahman woman.

33 An adulterer.

34 A gabbler.

35 One in the habit of using intoxicating drugs.

36 One who being a Brahman may were blue coloured dress.

37 One who takes alms from Muleches[1] and Chundals.[2]

If such persons be fed at "Saradh" the deceased ancestors for whose relief the Saradh feast is given go empty and unsatisfied, weeping and cursing the person who celebrates the ceremony.

Hearing this the Gooroo said O Shastree Brother, it is very difficult to act according to the Veda's rules; a person who does act this way is very rare; however the deceased ancestors are saved by that Saradh ceremony, which is performed at Teeruth and in which poor strangers are fed.

At the end of this discourse the Gooroo asked the Brahman about Sootuk[3] in answer of which one Pundit

---

[1] and [2] The meanest and obscure castes in India.

[3] Uncleanness produced by the birth of a child.

Devraj recited the Himadree Shaster to the Gooroo for one month. The Boodha Sahib said, O seikhs I had forgotten to relate this before, but even I do not think it necessary to do so. The Sahib Singh then said, O Sir, tell us a little on this subject also, from whom will the seikhs ask. The Boodha Sahib said, that the Gooroo had related to him about what Pundit Devraj had said and he remembered the following things out of that, viz. A Brahman remain unclean for ten days on account of a child's birth in his family.

A Brahman woman for 20 days.

A Khutree for 12 days.

A Bais for 15 days.

A Shooder for 30 days.

A Cow for 10 days.

A Female buffalo for 12 days.

The cow's and buffalo's milk should not be used in Jug Saradh or in preparing food for the gods before the expiring of so many days as are appointed above for their cleanness. If a man does so, he will be caught in worldly illness. Pátuk[1] washes off with it the uncleanness of Sootuk, but Sootuk does not wash of the uncleanness of Pátuk. The performance of fire ceremonies washes off the impurity of both Sootuk and Pátuk. One who being unclean on account of Sootuk or Pátuk gives charity to the Brahman goes to hell, and the Brahman who takes such a charity becomes a monkey in his next birth. A Brahman should not take the following kinds of charity :—

1 Charity given in Saradh performed at the time of eclipse.

2 Charity given by a sick man in order to get rid from his illness.

---

[1] Uncleanness produced by the occurrence of a death in the family.

3 Charity given by a man, who is at the point of death.

4 Charity given in funeral obsequies of a dead man.

5 Charity given in Sootuk.

One who goes to Teeruth, but does not give charity nor performs Saradh according to Veda's rules, becomes a Chundal in his next birth and there enjoys what he had given in an irregular way of charity. At the time of an eclipse and the birth of a son all waters become as holy as Ganges water. At the time of marriage a man should perform "Nundee Mookh Saradh," for by doing this he is saved from troubles and mournings. A man does not become unclean on account of Sootuk or Pátuk when he be in calamity or extreme pleasure or away at a distance or ignorant of the fact. If a clean Brahman does not discharge his religious duties, he becomes liable to all the evils. A covetous Brahman is a sinner. A covetous relative and a covetous pupil are sinners, and shall be sent to hell after which they will become evil spirits. This do the Vedas and Rishes say. The persons of all castes are my seikhs, hence I appoint 15 days for Sootuk. A day of Piturs[1] is equal to half of lunar month, or 15 days so I adopt the same i. e. I also appoint 15 days for Sootuk. An illiterate man and an uncovetous learned are good, but a learned sinner who panteth after wealth is a hellish being. Sakhee 75th finished.

SAKHEE SEVENTY-SIXTH.

Once when the Gooroo had returned from hunting, many devotees came to see him. At that time a banker of Dukkun Resident Ojain city also came. He was a Vaishnav[2] and had a wife and children. The Gooroo had

[1] Deceased ancestors.

[2] Worshippers of Vishnoo who do not eat flesh and wine.

many deers &c. killed around him and was enjoying giving meat to his hawk, when the banker saw him, the banker seeing this felt disgusted and had his belief changed, saying in his mind, why has the Gooroo become so unmerciful ? The Gooroo miracuously knowing his secrets said, O Seikh, about 1000 years ago that this Hawk was a king, and the killed animal was a thief and had stolen the property of the Rajah. The Rajah arrested him but the thief denied and swore falsely by me, who was a devotee at that time. The Rajah being my seikh trusted the thief's swearing and left him, so it is on account of that sin, that I feed this Hawk with the animals flesh. O my seikhs, one who swears falsely will die and be born again and again millions of times and will suffer the pains of hell. That animal now will be relieved from his sins. O Brothers one who swears falsely by the Gooroo is not my seikh. It is also bad to swear on truth, much more on falsehood. One who swears on truth shall be punished, how will the one who swears falsely be saved ? The Gooroo has become surety, but still the sin will be punished. O seikhs it is a natural thing to be in pleasure or sorrow, but you should always abstain from sin, in the meantime the Gooroo's dish was brought before him. The Gooroo ordered that banker of Dukkun to be fed with vegetable food prepared in a clean place. The banker was pleased to hear this as he was afraid of eating animal food. The banker then took his meals and went to his bed, as it was night. When he was lying down he said to himself, "I have brought 500 Rs. for the Gooroo, but why did my father adopt such a Gooroo, who eats flesh, for it is said that a devotee should abstain from killing, adultery, gaming and wine. It is better that I may leave this place in the morning and be a seikh of some Vishnav. My father sent 100 Rs. for the Gooroo, and told me to give 500 Rs. from my pocket. But I do not care for the money, no matter if my father had ordered me to pay 1000 Rs. more, but he should have sent me to a virtuous Gooroo." In these thoughts the morning came and arising from his bed bowed before the Gooroo, who ordered two bottles to be brought. At that time one Hurgopal a simple seikh of the Gooroo was present. The Gooroo said, O seikh it is mind that tastes. Some of the seikhs said, no king it is tongue that tastes, some said it is actions that tastes, some said it is soul that tastes, some said it is disposition that tastes, some said it is body that tastes, after all the banker seikh said, all depends upon the belief of the soul. The seikhs then told him on behalf of the Gooroo, "your father Bishumber Dass was a very faithful seikh of ours, you should tell him that we have accepted 100 Rs. sent by him. The banker said, O Gooroo explain me this, I am also your seikh. The Gooroo then laughed and said, you are Vishnav's pupil, how can you become our seikh; better look for a merciful and virtuous Gooroo; but your father will understand this message of ours. The banker then fell upon the Gooroo's feet and said, protect me O Gooroo, do not leave me, my mind is stupid, I did not know you. The Gooroo said, O Brother, I never became angry or displeased, go! I have forgiven thee, After this at the time of departure, the Gooroo granted Prashad[1] to the banker and ordered him to distribute it in his house. The Gooroo also granted him an iron bangle and said that by worshipping it the Gooroo will fulfil his desires. The banker taking the Prashad and iron-bangle departed. Sakhee 76th finished.

SAKHEE SEVENTY-SEVENTH.

The abovesaid banker as he was going said to himself, "I have given 600 Rs. to the Gooroo, but he has

[1] E. B.

only given me some Karah Prashad and an iron-bangle, besides this he recited me the words of divine love and then allowed me to depart. Thinking this way he arrived in Chumkour. While he was thinking this way on his way, he met one Dhian Singh, who asked him about his whereabouts and told him to be his (Dhian Singh's guest) The banker told him that he was a native of Ojain and had returned after seeing the Gooroo, whom he had given heavy present, but was not pleased to see his (Gooroo's) habits nor had the Gooroo granted him any thing. Dhian Singh asked him of what the Gooroo had taught him and he replied that the Gooroo had only sent the "word of love" for his father by him. Dhian singh told him not to repent but as he was his religious brother he should go to eat and put up in his house. Saying this Dhian Singh took him to his house and both he and his wife served him very well. In the morning when he was going Dhian Sing told him that if he likes, he can sell the Gooroo's word and take 600 Rs. from him, but that he would not advice him to do so, as the Gooroo's precept was that his seikhs should not cheat their guests, so in the first place he would advise him (the banker) to take the word to his house, but if he loved the money he can take the sum from him, The banker said that he believed in the money and that he would sell the word to him, if he (Dhian Singh) would pay him 550 Rs. Hearing this, Dhian Sing arose and mortgaging all his property, wife and children brought 600 Rs. with 5 Rs. extra as interest and paid the total 605 to the banker, who was pleased and said to himself, behold! Dhian Singh the fool, have lost and I have won! The banker then set out to his journey. Sakhee 77th finished.

SAKHEE SEVENTY-EIGHTH.

On proceeding further, the banker opend his baggage and saw that the Karah Prashad was turned into the cooked flesh; seeing this, he felt disgusted and became extremely displeased with his father, saying, what a flesh-eating Gooroo my father has adopted. "It is a sin to eat flesh." On going further he bought 1,000 Rs. worth jewels and sold them in the city called "Pallee," making a profit of 2,000 Rs. on the bargain. The banker then arrived at his house and boasted of his bargain before his father, whom he also said, "I am subject to your will, tell me how have you belived in the Gooroo." Saying this he placed before him the Gooroo's Prashad, which was found quite fresh and delicious, though eaten two months after its preparation. The Bishumber (his father) then put the Karah Prashad on his head, distributed it in his house and ate it himself. The banker then related all the past wonders relating to the Karah Prashad i. e. the fact if its being turned into the cooked flesh &c., &c. The father then moved his head and said, O my son tell me truly, I had sent you to gain something, but it appears that you have bought glass-beads for me, you have not done this well! notwithstanding you have seen Gooroo's miracles with your own eyes. An impure mind cannot know of the excellence of the Gooroo's habits. Hearing this the banker in the presence of his father became angry with his mother and said, "My true Gooroos are my parents." Here my words attentively. I was not pleased, I sold the Gooroo's words and bought the jewels, so I have earned 3,000 Rs. which will be of some use to me. Of what use were the Gooroo's words! You the simple persons disrespected me and did not admire my wisdom, which is a good one. Hearing this the father said O my son hear me, my Gooroo is complete but your wisdom is dull, do not speak ill of the Gooroo, you and

I will be happy by touching the Gooroo's feet. All this wealth is deceiving do not love it. The man is only to live but few days, understand fully what I say. The banker hearing this remained silent and the love of the Gooroo was not produced in his heart. Bishumber, his father, kept quiet and understanding that the clamity was coming over them wept before his wife. The banker opened a shop and his wealth began to increase, so that he became the owner of 10,000 Rs. which made him a very fat man. After sometime his wealth began to decrease and he being reduced to poverty fell upon his father's feet, whom he took together with the rest of his household to the Gooroo. In the way he put up with all his relatives in the house of Dhian Singh of "Majra" who treated them very hospitably and gave them food to eat. In the night Bishumber said, O Dhian Singh, it has been well known that you bought the Gooroo's word from my son. What shall be my condition now! Please recommend me to the Gooroo and asssist me as you are my spiritual brother. In the morning, Dhian Singh, the banker and all his relatives went and fell upon the feet of the kind and generous Gooroo, who seing them laughed and gave them delicious foods to eat. They lived there for three days. Bishumber recommended his son to the Gooroo and applied that his sins may be forgiven, saying, that O Gooroo, you are like a seed and we as the crooked branches of the tree, please make us straight. You are kind and we are great sinners and we of perverse understanding. The Gooroo seeing them in this condition laughed and said Baba Nanuk had also gone to your house in previous ages. At that time your name was Baba Nanoo, who was a man of good actions. You wanted to ask a question from Baba Nanuk, who laughed and ordered you to give the 10th part of your earnings in charity and told you to ask this question in your future birth. So O dear, you are the same Baba Nanoo and I am Baba Nanuk, now ask your questions. I was willing to see you and therefore there is no fault of your son. Boodha Sahib then said that Bishumber asked the nice question from the Gooroo in his presence. The Dhian Singh who had bought the Gooroo's word found treasure in the earth and thus became a rich man. He offered the Gooroo so much of that treasure as remained after paying off his debts. The Gooroo ordered him to enjoy it as it was the result of his true and strong faith. The Gooroo further said, wherever God's will is, there the rain falls and that thundering in the sky is merely a fun. You O Dhian Singh and the banker are equal, in the morning I will tell you about the desire of serving.

On the following day the Gooroo asked the seikh, Bishumber, what do you want you are purified by my feet, there is no one like you in the South. Bishumber first asked for riches and for his redemption from the cares of the world. The Gooroo laughed and said, when you will go to your house you should prepare "Karah Prashad" and putting it covered before you, you should read "Anund Sahib" thrice and the whole of Jupjee one time. Then you should distribute a part of this to five seikhs and give five shares for the Gooroo, after reading "Ardass" beforehand. Without "Ardass," what is the use of Munter,[1] repeating the sacred names &c. &c. The good effect is produced by "Ardass" only O devotees whoever is a seikh, should make religious trade and the Gooroo will give him a profit. He should call his seikh brother and give "Kurah prashad" to him. Hearing this the seikh said, O Gooroo our country is ears, i. e. as we hear so we do. Please tell us in detail about the "Ardass," that the seikhs may obtain comfort. Hearing this the Gooroo said, a man should prepare "Karah Prashad" of Sugar or black Sugar, but if he could not pro-

---

[1] E. B.

vide for his he should bring fruits, after making himself pure by bathing &c., then he should engage himself in worship for the whole day. Thus through the effect of God's name he will obtain success in his undertaking. By hearing the voice of "Ardass," the seed of virtue springs up, the faith becomes fruitful, the plant of comfort brings forth fruit and the heart of the seikh overflows with joy. On the 8th of the lunar month, a man should give desired food and some cloth in charity and should divide and eat himself the same sort of food. On the 10th day after this, he should feed the children and should please them very much. At this time he should cause the "Ardass" to be read. He should not take meals in his own house at the time of Sootuk or three days of woman's menses. If he will do so, he will become sick, at such a time he should eat in Gooroo's institution. He should read the "Ardass,"[1] or prayer, in the following way, viz., O God, join the people in happy sports, they may love the repetition of your name, their tongue may utter the name of the Gooroo, they may love to undergo the "Pahool"[2] ceremony, the wicked may be put to flight, the seikhs may roar like a lion, the edge of the sword and javelin may remain sharp, the lion (i. e. a seikh) may get a patient horse, the deer-like wicked may be attacked together, by your favor trouble may be put off and the rest obtained, thy orders may be received and acted upon, the body may be increased and the sorrow diminished the true Gooroo, the Chief, may reign completely, I have offered this thing for the true Gooroo, who has kept my faith strong, may the love of Gooroo be complete in my heart, the thief may become blind, the Gooroo may keep me engaged in the household business, may cause me to be acquainted with a king, may protect me

[1] Ardass is a special prayer read at the time when an offering is made to the seikh or Hindoo institutions. In this the priest generally announces blessings to one who has brought the present.

[2] Baptism of seikhs.

himself may cause the rain to fall and may root out the famine; I am a transgressor of the path of comfort, please forgive and make me to go on good ways. May my deceased ancestors get rest and the lion-like heart may be subjected. O true Gooroo forgive!!

This "Ardass" consisting of thirty prayers has been taught by the Gooroo, whoever will hear it attentively will be saved from pain and hunger and the true Gooroo will always keep him satisfied. Sakhee 78th finished.

SAKHEE SEVENTY-NINTH.

Hearing the above "Ardass," the seikh fell upon the feet of the Gooroo, who was pleased and said, may you live long with your wife. I explain you all things fully. You will get rid from the trouble. All the other religions will be destroyed and the wicked will perish. A man will be saved from the effect of ghosts, the Martyrs will protect him. At the time of sleeping a man should read the 34th prayer out of the following prayers :—

34 May I get rest.

35 May the Gooroo increase animals and every thing.

36 May I love the "Ardass" and have faith in it.

37 May the Ardass bring forth fruit and useless things be fruitful.

38 May the head of my enemy be bent and the building of a new house be begun.

39 May the beginners of Ardass become-strong.

40 May the field remain safe, I will be obliged by this.

41 May not the earth and heaven perish.

42 May the true Gooroo give riches and the power of eight sorts of miracles.

43 May the Gooroo protect our honor and our faith.

44 May our private works be done.

45 May I be known to public when I go out of my house.

46 Please patronise your pupil, while entangled in the care of household business.

47 You are the only person who can keep up the sufficiency of the income of the treasury.

48 The diseases may be cured and the enemy annihilated by the favor of the Gooroo.

49 Join the separated, O Gooroo, I was entangled in a great net. The learned men know it.

50 The practice of cheating may be abolished and the people may rejoice.

51 May thy Durbar be opened and may we obtain desired enjoyments.

52 The Gooroo has granted the power of fighting without a stranger's help and an elephant, we understand all our works done and pay homage to thee.

53 Enable us to abstain from woman's bed, when she be in her monthly courses, and give us patience to prevent the temptation.

54 May the "Ashonee[1] Koowar" grant us the strength of mind.

55 The marriage ceremonies may be begun and the seikh be blessed by your favor.

56 Strike out the evil thoughts of a seikh entangled in worldly cares.

---

[1] The Medical Professor of the gods in Hindoo mythology.

57 May the enchanting powers of seikhs be pleasing to the spectator and the works of the seikhs be done.

58 In singing sacred songs, may the name of the true Gooroo be repeated and may I hear the praise of the Gooroos' name.

59 May the Martyr seikhs prevent me from following that way which is opposite to seikhism.

60 May the heart of mine become humble and meek when I visit sages and devotees and may such visits be fruitful for me.

These 60 prayers are fitted to import blessings and rejoicings. I have taught you these O Bishumber, my seikh, for your love towards me is great and I have not seen any other person like you! Sakhee 79th finished.

---

* SAKHEE EIGHTIETH.

61 May the heart of mine become straight and keep me safe from the pit of the world.

62 May the heart and attention be fixed in the Gooroos' feet.

63 May I not be entangled in the love of women.

64 May I always consider myself as the servant and slave of the Gooroo.

65 May the faith remain true and may the Gooroo protect.

66 May the body remain in comfort and ease.

67 May the Gooroo make the Sugarcane sweet.

68 May I be the master of the pantry of the world and may I be the lover of seikhs.

69 May the faith be strong and may the attention be drawn to divine love.

---

* The chain of prayers is extended to this Sakhee also as far as No. 75.

70 May the fire and sun strengthen my body in battle.

71 May I remain healthy and comfortable both day and night.

72 Rear your seikh up in palanquin and keep him in ease for ever.

73 May the Gooroo annihilate our sins.

74 May the Burn[1] guard us in large quantity of waters.

75 May we be in the habit of binding our turbans straight.

After reciting these prayers, the Gooroo said, O Bishumber, thou art my friend and pure seikh. The seikh is my worship. A seikh should maintain and pay attentiou to his own form. The seikh is a mine of comforts. O Bishumber hear me, keep aside five farthings every day for the Gooroo, and you will become wealthy. I have granted you wealth. Your attention will be drawn to luxuries and wealth, but you should try to teach the ignorant seikhs whether males or females about myself. The words of the Gooroo are the words of the gods. You should be attached strictly to the routine of daily duties dictated by the Gooroo. You should first bathe for three hours, make divine worship and after that engage yourself in household business. You should speak as little as possible and speak the truth whenever and wherever you speak. This will annihilate your trouble and pains. It is easy to subject the mind. We should first subject our body, be true in our dealings and live according to the Gooroo's precepts. A seikh should give up discussion should not be entangled in the love of wealth and sons, and make his habits and words straight. The Gooroo's precept is that a seikh should shun the society

[1] God of waters.

of those who are proud and heard-speaking, and who kill their daughters. A seikh should not accept the counsel of women and should not make himself the friend of boys. A seikh should not dwindle his mind in battle and should discharge his duties with pleasure. Saying this, the Gooroo was pleased to make Hurgopal, the son of Bishumber, a seikh by Churn[1] Pahool ceremony.

Now hear what the true Gooroo has ordered his seikh to do. Sakhee 80th finished.

SAKHEE EIGHTY-FIRST.

Bishumberdass again asked the Gooroo saying, O Gooroo if we cannot get a faithful seikh, how should we perform the "Churn pahool" ceremony? The Gooroo answered, "my seikh should on such an occasion believe in my words, nourish the love of my feet, may know the ten Gooroos as of equal position, may think the "First Grunth Sahib" as the 11th Gooroo (apart from that Gooroo who teaches precepts) and may perform the "Churn Pahool" ceremony by drinking the water with which the handkerchief of Grunth Sahib may be washed. This water should be taken from the hands of any Gooroo. Doing this way the seikh should make his belief firm and distribute "Karah Prashad" to the people. The Gooroo then may give him name according to the 11th verse or according to the Grunth's almanac. He should use the beautiful word "Sree" over and over again. He should discharge his home duties keeping his faith in the Gooroo's house. He should marry his daughter with an humble seikh. The seikh of both ceremonies should leave the world. The seikh of "Churn

---

[1] Ex. Before.

pahool"[1] should give his daughter in marriage to the seikh of "Khundapahool" and the latter should accept it. When a seikh of Khunda Pahool may not be found he may give his daughter in marriage to his equals, for there is no difference between lips and the teeth, or between the father and son. Likewise there is no difference between the Gooroo and seikh, between two sorts of "Pahools" and between the old and young. A seikh should take "Pahool" from whomsoever he thinks fit, without any regard to the castes. Such a seikh is a nice man. The seikhs should love and exchange presents with each other. They should eat and give debts to each other. Once, who being a seikh will cheat another, shall and get no place to stand. A seikh should always love the name of God, should repeat the name, should devote himself to the name, should teach the name and should understand the name as the only comfort for him. The life of that man who is the friend of the name is blessed, and blessed is the man, who behaves according to the Gooroo's precepts, eats only for the sake of maintaining his body, is disinterested in the world as a traveller in journey, and remains always active. O seikh hear attentively the way of departure, I and you both will depart from this world. No one is saved from death. This, however, is said for the sake of producing disinterestedness in the world; in fact, no one ever dies or is born. The pure soul is from the beginning and remains in the end. This life is like a dream. These are the instructions of "Yoga" science, O Brother, which I have related to you. Fifteen sorts of "yoga" practices are performed for the sake of "Sohung[2] Hunsa" and the true Gooroo supports all sorts of breath. The sound of Anhud[3]

---

[1] The piece of cloth in which the "Grunth Sahib" or the sacred Book of the seikh is wrapped.

[2] A technicality of "Yoga" science representing something divine, but it cannot be fully explained.

[3] Sound heard at the time of shutting up the holes of both.

is heard at the time of repeating the name of true Gooroo, on whom we should contemplate in secret. The four precious things are in the hands of the Gooroo, the fifth one is this "Ardass," (the abovesaid prayer), The 6th completeness, the detector of cheat will satisfy our desires. The 7th is that the true Gooroo grants all desired objects to one who seeks his protection. The 8th is that a man should believe in truth and turn the beads of Rosary. The 9th is that the Gooroo is worthy of being worshipped and able to save from hell. The 10th is that a man should not burn himself and should be satisfied with little. O seikh, you should not be superstitious, your duty is to believe in one thing, Sutgoor[1] is the protector of his seikhs, as the habits of purity and divine love protect people from those who are powerful.

15 The words of love should be obeyed, this is the way of the true Gooroo by treating others respectfully, man's soul is flourished, the relatives become peaceful, wisdom reaches to a great height and the family life becomes fruitful. This is the beautiful way of living.

23rd The Gooroo's quiver, and

24th The Gooroo's dagger, do not fail to kill the enemy.

25th A seikh may live with honor in the house of the Gooroo.

26th A seikh may become old in living near the Gooroo.

Thus the pains of 100 years pass away by means of these hundred prayers. The Gooroo bears witness to this fact. When the Gooroo may put up in the seikhs house, he should receive the 10th part of his (Seikhs) earnings, and the seikh should also worship the feet of "Ardassi" or one who reads prayers for him, when the

---

[1] Meaning the true Gooroo.

offering is made to the Gooroo. That seikh who gives the 10th part of his earnings to the Gooroo with the repetition of "Ardass," adopts the customs and manners of seikhism, abstains from the bed of a woman, who is not legally married with him and from coveting another man's wealth, believes in the Gooroo's feet and reads Gooroo's words, is saved from the pains of births and deaths." Sakhee 81st finished.

SAKHEE EIGHTY-SECOND.

The Gooroo further continued to say, "My Seikh should not shave head at the death of his parents, nor should he mourn or weep for a deceased relative. He should save himself from bad actions and lead his family to good ways. He should not sell fruits nor should carry on trade in corn, grass, fuel and leather. He should not lend money to Chundál and mean fellows nor should borrow money from prostitutes. He should not quarrel, nor should inflame the anger in his bosom. He should not sit in the square of a street and should not use the broken vessels or broken couch. He should first wash half his feet and then the mouth and should scour his teeth with the sand. He should not laugh when eating and should rub his hand on the body after taking meals. It is never good to laugh or weep before the Gooroo, for by so doing the wealth is destroyed and poverty comes. It is not good to eat bread in the way nor it is good to ease one's self or to piss on the road every day. A seikh should not touch the cow and the Brahman with feet, nor should he speak ill of the food that has been eaten. In solitude he should engage himself in the religious contemplations and should not feel anxiety in his heart for future things. He should not make friendship with the bad women or the Policemen. He should not be waking for the whole night, nor should have sexual intercourse many times in a night. He should leave away the lazy messenger, the lewd seikh, and the raw and dry flesh. He should not think of defaming or backbiting and should bring his senses under his subjection. He should not say in his heart that he would not suffer any man to be proud, atheist or backbiter before him. He should pass his days in the world like a bird on the tree. He should be disinterested in the wealth and riches. He should understand that his soul is quite separate from his body. He should hear the Shasters and be not proud. He should not bind himself in the love of any thing, but should by and by diminish his burden till he gets rid of the whole. He should teach good morals and wise precepts to the people. He should apply himself in the practice of purifying and confining his breaths. He should not be late in taking meals and should not praise the food of "Sootuk" and the beauty of another man's wife, nor should he enjoy them. He should not sit in the society of foolishmen, Wrestlers and rope-dancers. He should bring up his son in the society of devotees and should not stop in a temple for a long time. He should inform no one of his secrecies and should view all equally. He should not be partial in administrating justice and should not be in the habit of talking on the subject of sensual pleasures and should not be panting for eating delicious foods. He should be in the habit of eating simple food and should be simple in his transactions. There remains no quarrel in the house of that man who behaves in this way. Sakhee 82nd finished.

SAKHEE EIGHTY-THIRD.

Dhian Singh after hearing these precepts from the Gooroo sold off all the property of his house. The Gooroo then said to a seikh who was sitting near, "See this man's belief." Hearing this Dhian Singh spoke, O Gooroo, when you become kind on me, my belief was confirmed; O Lord, I have been enriched and happy since the day I bought your word from "Hurgopal Bunya. On the 7th day after that I began to plough my land when suddenly I found a treasure in the ground. My mind had first swollen with pleasure, but was soon after reduced to its former state. Coming to my house I prepared and distributed "Karah Prashad" for the Gooroo and fed all the poor Brahmans that I could find. I brought the rest before you on the 10th day and told you that it was your property how should I treat with it? you told me that it was the profit of my trade and that I had given the tenth part of it for the Gooroo. I then returned to my house and began to do beneficial acts with that money. It has been very well that this seikh Bishumber, has come with his son and has presented himself before your feet. He is a good virtuous seikh and his faults have now been forgiven and his troubles and diseases annihilated. He has adopted you as a Gooroo in the place of a "Vashnav" Gooroo and is now standing before you as the servant of your feet. He has not been broken in heart nor enfeebled in spirits. He is a simple seikh and has been sealed by Gooroo Nanuk. He has accepted sword "Pahool" ceremony to destroy Mahammedans; saying this Dhian Singh called the son of Bishumber and told him, O seikh, thou art the limit of the faith, my love is increased towards you, I had advised your father Bishumber, but you have advised your mind. At that time the Gooroo laughed and told Dhian Singh to ask something from him, as he (the Gooroo) was pleased with his faith and considered him as a part of his body. Dhian Singh then, said O Gooroo, you have now granted the word of kindness, but how shall it happen in future, perhaps seikh's faith may fade, so better grant me the strong faith only. The Gooroo laughed and said O Sahib

Singh, hear my word, the ocean, Lusnia[1] Diamond and the Pearl will go to a low place only. My body is like the sun, when it shall not exist, shall be dark all over the world. The fire-worms will arise and will light the world and my seikhs shall be suppressed. I have given my seikhs the faith, the wealth, and the complete knowledge. They shall become heroes and giving up falsehood, shall go to be kings and being mounted on the back of adorned elephants they shall accept the faith granted by me. Sakhee 83rd finished.

SAKHEE EIGHTY-FOURTH.

Once the Gooroo was sitting after the morning ablutions and other people, men and women were bathing when some of the seikhs asked, O true king, why do the people bathe early in the morning in the months of Katuk and Magh and why do they bathe in rain sometimes? The Gooroo replied, O Brother this world is a fun, what reason can be given for these things. When the cow gives milk, people understand it as the God's favor, and while they are worshipping gods their minds are fixed in the city. The woman who brings forth sons is loved. If a Jujman pays money to his Brahman, the Brahman likes him. If the master feeds his servants well, the servant's heart is pleased. If the husband does not earn any thing the wife is disgusted in her heart. The people blindly follow each other. O my seikhs, the God always is pleased with the true love, hear from me those precepts, which if acted upon, give the fruit of a yoga (Public feast) every day and increase the faith of seikhs in the Gooroo. If a man bathes at 3 o'clock in the night he earns the blessings of Ahomed and Gowmed Yogas. If a man bathes a Ghuree later, he earns the blessings of worshipping fire.

---

[1] A sort of Diamond.

If a man bathes two Ghurees later he earns the blessings of some yoga." If a man bathes three Ghurees later he earns the blessings of giving gold in charity. If a man bathes four Ghurees latter he earns the blessings of giving silver in charity. If a man bathes five Ghurees later he earns the blessings of giving copper in charity. If a man bathes six Ghurees later he earns the blessings of giving milk in charity. If a man bathes at sunrise, his sins are forgiven. If a man bathes at noon, he is merely purified. If a man bathes in the afternoon his bathing is like a Malech's bathing. If a man bathes in the evening, that bathing is the sign of wrath of God. If a man bathes in the midnight, he is a sinner. If a man does not bathe at all, he is as great a sinner as slaughterer of all the living beings. These are the rules of bathing. A man should after bathing, repeat the name of "Ram" and this will save him. One who is of true habits, gets ease, and the variety of puzzling ceremonies is a false show. The Argha[1] is a bait hook and the names a net. If the true Gooroo be pleased, he should grant a man true habits. such a man remains happy in the world. O brother it is easy to be saved by these ways. A man should always apply himself to good and virtuous actions and should not be a slave of worldly pleasures. A man should in this manner pass his days in the world. The businesses of the world are merely amusements and give no use, such as, playing at chess, cards, chounper and Ram chouk is useless and without profit. Here ends the 84th Sakhee.

SAKHEE EIGHTY-FIFTH.

After this the Gooroo continued to say O Seikh Brothers, Divine love is the chief thing! That man says the Veda in whose body there is a torrent of divine love,

[1] A vessel with which Hindoos give water to their deceased ancestors after bathing.

is holy and comfortable. A man without love is like "Hurnakus" and "Hurn-Kushub demons. It was for the sake of love that God appeared in the body of "Nurshing' Awtar." "Lahus Baboo" dewan had no love and was hence killed by "Parasram." "Rawan" was killed because he had no love. One who has stout body and loud voice should not, even by inadvertence, remember any other person except God. That God is within you, O seikhs, as butter is in the curds and electricity in the stone. That God shines every where, likewise. He shines in you, but you cannot know it unless you are freed from the bondage of worldly cares and absorbed in divine love, but one who has known him is truly happy. The God is truth, living and omnipresent like sky; and one who shines with his own light and never perishes, he is happy within himself and acts every day according to his own will, by knowing this a man obtains his desires. This world is an illusion and has no real existence in any of the three tenses.[2] It is a mere name like the horns of a hare, son of a barren, flowers of the sky and the mirage. O Bishumber, my dear seikh, may your desires be obtained and the bounds of the births and deaths broken. There are eight births heavy over your head. Bishumber then asked, O true Gooroo, tell me of my future birthplace, may I live near you wherever I live and be your slave everywhere. Hearing this the Gooroo said, it is good to be virtuous, O Bishumber you should read "Bhoput Nama" or the following names of the Gooroos and then you will live as absorbed in me. The names are :—

1 Baba Nanuk Sahib.
2 Gooroo Augal.
3 The glorious Gooroo Amardass.
4 Gooroo Ramdass.

An incarnation of Deity resembling both lion and man.
Past, present and future.

5 Gooroo Argun.

6 Gooroo Hurgobind, the beautiful.

7 Gooroo Hur Rai.

8 Gooroo Hur Kishen.

9 Gooroo Tegh Bahadur.

10 And his son, I the Gooroo Gobind Singh whom you are now seeing before you.

I will come to you to fulfil God's will, when I will leave this body and appear in my next body. I and you will be born in the city of Gooroo Ramdass, the 3rd person "Goordas will you join us? You will be my counsellor and we shall devise good plans and will be born in Amritsur[1] in the Sub 1900. We shall learn the military science of "Khutrees" for thirteen years. I shall be the only son of my mother in Aikulsut family. That man will be the 10th part of my essence and being born in the Punjab will be a happy being. When I. shall be sixteen years of age I will conquer the west. In the Sub 1914 I will conquer Kabool. I will marry and will not show my face to anybody. I will kill my enemies and will sit on the throne of Delhie. There (in Delhie) is a Teeruth called "Nigum Bodh" wherein I will bathe and leaving my that body will be born again in the Majha[2] country. I will then marry with great difficulty, will join the separated persons, and will forgive the faults of my seikhs, I will relate to you all things in detail and will dispel all the doubts from your heart. Goorbux Singh Ramkour shall die in Kanshee for me, in his second birth and shall become my prince. I will kill all and will make him to enjoy the pleasures of the world. Be careful, one who is a man of good habits in my religion will be saved from the pains of the regions of the God of death. All the chiefs will then follow me and

[1] Amritsur.

[2] Lahore and Amritsur territory.

will fight battles by plundering people. I will then take back millions of Rupees which were deposited by me in the water. The ocean will give this money to me through Mowns. At that time a mountainer my enemy will keep the treasures for increase then in Sub 1897. In Sub 1890 there shall be a famine in the country. In the Sub 1900, I will nourish the body of Soordass. At that time there shall be eighteen incarnations of the devotees. At that time I will attack Delhie, my Sungat will be both in trouble and ease. The Englishmen shall vex the people and shall according to the laws of policy suppress my religions. On that day I shall perform a wonder. A little fighting will ensue, the success will follow my incantations, the Englishmen shall be driven to middle countries, and my "Bhoojungee" seikhs will roar again. Hearing this the seikh asked the meaning of the word "Bhoojungee" and the kind Gooroo replied, Seikh follow Bhai Oudu Singh's habits. In the house of Kesho Dass Brahman a beautiful woman shall become Mahammedan by force and the chief will enjoy Mahammedan prostitutes. In his house a lustful white-man shall be born and shall be called Bhoojungee, which word as used in Vedas is Toorungee. He shall be as powerful as a male. Now O Brother hear what shall come to pass. A seikh will enjoy an English woman, at that time heat of seikh's roaring will be felt. Hear what good things shall come to pass. No one shall reach this position. In every house learned men, devotees and rich men shall repeat the name of God. In the cities of Kanshee, Delhie and Kundhar, money will be collected and spent. I will then appear as an incarnation of virtue, will enjoy the pleasures and will refresh my mind. Such will be my way of living. There shall be no mourning and lustful love of women and O Brother, a rare person shall know me. One of my sons shall be born in "Patul" * city and another shall be born in the house of a Rajpoot.

* Patulah.

This second son shall be driven out of the Fort of Kangra and shall die on Ganges' banks. He will then again be born in my religion and shall conquer kingdoms. A servant of mine shall conquer the Khanshee city and shall be devoted to the worship of "Shiva." A Rajah of Jummoo city shall advise my seikhs and shall take taxes from all countries. The Khalsa will follow him in the hills and being spread on the surface of 3000 miles, the Khalsa will cause great disturbance. The seikhs will take the yellow fort and will protect the four castes. When it shall be Sub 96[1] they shall conquer Persia and Kundhar. In the Sub 97[2] the army of the east shall rise and one Sooruj of Goojur caste shall come into existence. There shall be two sorts of my servants, viz, Gilje and Mahammedans, Dogar and Englishmen. The Khutree and Brahman shall be my seikhs and Dya Singh will be born second time. In the Sub 1900 I will establish the kingdom in order and will reach soon in the Kulkpoori.[3] My birth place is Patna city. I shall see these things as a dream in the night. I will take taxes from some persons and will usurp the kingdoms of others. I will conquer all those countries which were travelled by Baba Nanuk in the dress of a religious mendicant. The credit of Khalsa will be increased and no one will recognize me. They shall view me as Rahoo[4] who devours the sun during an eclipse. The most loving following seikhs, viz., Jhunda Singh, Gunda Singh, Sooja Singh,. Sookha Singh, Nam Singh, Dan Singh, Boodha Singh, Siam Sing, Loodh Singh, Sahib Singh and Nowrung Singh shall be born in "Patul[5] Nuger." How far shall I relate the future things, which are pleasing to my seikhs. My servant the son of a Ma-

---

[1] 1896

[2] 1897

[3] Probably meant Calcutta.

[4] A Star in the heavens who is supposed by Hindoos to devour the sun and moon during an eclipse.

[5] Patialah.

hammedan will conquer the west and will follow my steps. One who will read the names of my abovesaid Rajahs, his body shall become pure and holy, no matter whether he reads it in the evening, morning, or night. That seikh who will read it in the morning, shall be saved from the evils of Kuliyoga. Go, O seikh, to thy residence, you shall be able to see both past and future, all your works shall be done rightly, and you shall be able to see me freely whenever you like. Sakhee 85th finished.

SAKHEE EIGHTY-SIXTH.

Boodha Sahib said, while the following account, O Sahib Singh, on the next morning, the true Gooroo ordered me to bring water for him and to call the Oojain seikhs four Ghurees[1] after the sunrise. I did so. The Oojainee seikh came with his son and presented the Gooroo with 1000 Rs. of "Shah Jahen" coin and was pleased to do so. The females of that seikh's family were with him and permission was given for them to come and worship the Gooroo. One of them a woman named "Muddenwuntee placed her head on the Gooroo's feet on which also fell the tears from her eyes. The Gooroo at that time had drawn back his feet but she had also proceeded further. The Gooroo then laughed and told her, do not be in care, the Gooroo's house gives, but does not take. Your son will be my servant in his next birth, but we have given him to thee in his present birth. This is proved but no one knows it, except Garunth or yourself. The seikh woman said, "may it be that I should not be entangled in the family love." The Gooroo said, be careful O Goorbux Sing's wife, you will repent for the sake of a son, for thy habits are like males, while thy sex is female. Hearing this the woman laughed and was pleased. After this the other

[1] An Indian hour equal to twenty-four minutes of English hour.

seikh woman called "Moodnee" bowed before the Gooroo who moved his head and remained silent. Then all the seikh women bowed and took leave of the Gooroo. After all the women had gone away the Gooroo laughed. Seeing the Gooroo pleased, I asked, what is the order O king. The Gooroo said, "Muddenwuntee shall be thy wife, and behold, I have given thee all the territory of Jawalajee to reign over, but your life will be of short duration. The Gooroo further addressed me, saying O young boy! why have you felt ashamed! What, seeing a beautiful woman you have become fond of her and you thought by inadvertence that I had not granted the woman to you! Behold I have granted the woman to you! and it shall be thine O Goobrux Sing. The other seikh woman being in her courses touched my feet, hence I did not speak with her nor touched her. It is so ordained by God that[1] this woman shall be a Mahammedan prostitute in her next birth, but through the faith she have had in me, she shall become a concubine of "Kesho Dass" Missur "Run † Singh." After that she shall be born in the house of a Hindoo Rajpoot and this time also I will grant her to my seikh Missur Keshodas in the same birth. The Gooroo then prevented me from asking further, saying that it was the time for him to be engaged in some other thought and I consequently kept quiet. Sakhee 86th finished.

SAKHEE EIGHTY-SEVENTH.

After this the Gooroo slept in the night. The next morning he collected the following Pundits and Poets, viz., Koower, Bulabh, Goonya, Sookhia &c. &c. and asked them the following questions, saying O Brother, what is

[1] And this woman has taken her birth, as according to the opinions and statement of many persons, in the Mahammedan race by the name of Maron, and she was a kept woman to Runjeet Sing.

† Here Runjeet Singh is to be known as Run Singh.

the dream and what is the cause of it? Why do the black marks appear in the moon? Why do persons put their Turban on the knee after binding it? Why do people spit after making water? Why do people speak when no one hears them? Why do the cookers break a little piece of dough and place it on the top of the mass? Why do people draw and sound the bow before they discharge an arrow? Why do they touch the tobacco? Why do they not read God's word on twelveth of the dark and light halves of the lunar month. Hearing this the Koowur Poet gave the following answers. viz.

1 The food we eat is digested and the price of it is such by the veins, which being filled push the mind into deep slumber, the true sense of the man is lost and the pictures of the imagination appear as true at that time. I know so much through my own impressions. You know the further.

2 After this Bulabh Poet said, "The moon had abetted Indra in committing adultery with Gautum Rishe's wife, hence his face has been scarred with black marks.

3 After this Goonya said, the Ganges has been produced from the knees of Jhunnoo Rishee, therefore the knee having been considered the good place, the turban which is the crown of the head is first put on it.

4 The Sookhia said, to avoid the effects of sorcery, people spit after making water, and become senseful.

5 The Goordass said, when a man comes to the protection of the Gooroo his pride is checked, but without your favor a man becomes so fool as to speak even when no one hears him.

6 The Sainaput said, in the beginning of everything "Gunesh" is worshipped, so a cooker also breaks a little

piece of dough as present for the Gunesh in the beginning of his cooking work.

7 The Sookha Sing said, by sounding the bow, we harangue the enemy and challenge them to fight. The Kulooya replied the 8th and 9th questions, saying.

8 It is on account of the Mahammedan reign that people have begun to touch the tobacco, as powers derived from divine worship and the effects of sacred incantations were to be annihilated, and this annihilation is caused by eating Jooth[1] which the seekers of tobacco cannot avoid.

9 The sins once complained before the Vishnoo, saying, that his (Vishnoo's) history annihilates them. The Vishnoo then told them that on the 12th day of the both halves of lunar month they could not be annihilated by his history.

Baba Nanuk says, with whom the God is pleased, his sins are forgiven, as the slave's son Bider, Soodhaman the poor, Ajamul the sinner, Koobja, and Bheelnee had their sins forgiven.

After this all kept silent. Then the Gooroo said, O Goor Bux Singh, why do you not speak. You should also say something.

The Goor Bux Singh then said, "My mind is fixed on your feet, what can we do, all things depend upon you the creator, I remember you day and night. Please save me, I know but you.

The Gooroo then laughed, hear O Sahib Singh. I then addressed the Gooroo with folded hands and entreated him to answer those questions himself for the good of his Sungat. Sakhee 87th finished.

---

[1] A thing which has become impure by another man's first using a part or whole of it by mouth.

SAKHEE EIGHTY-EIGHTH.

The Gooroo then made the following replies of the preceeding questions.

1 The soul being at rest in the sleep, sees those things which he ever seen in his previous births.

2 The moon had committed adultery with Tara, the wife of Brahsputi Gooroo, hence his face has been scarred with black marks. The God has thus convinced the people that adultery is a great sin.

3 Once Ram and Luchmun, two Brothers, went out to hunt and were separated in the forest. The night approached, and each of them in order to amuse the heart put his turban on the knee and supposing it as a second friend, conversed with him and thus passed the night easily. In the morning when they met each other they blessed the method by which they had amused themselves last night and said that man will be saved from trouble by putting turban on the knee this way.

4 The evil spirits on the ground are annihilated when a person makes water and the body becomes clean by spitting.

5 When a man is grasped by the sin it stupifies his senses and he begins to talk when no one hears him.

6 The family men pluck off a little bit of dough as God's share according to Veda's words.

7 By sounding the bow all heroes are awakened and take it as a good and the Gods by doing this come on the right hand of the person sounding the bow in the presence of his enemy.

8 Ajmeer Shaw had a daughter, and that daughter used to bring Mandub Rishee every night per force, to

pass the night with her. But the said Mandub Rishee by the influence of some "*Muntur*" could secure himself from committing any act of criminal violation and the daughter of Ajmeer Shaw was totally powerless to come to the same bed with the Rishee. But the Gooroo of Ajmeer Shaw, advised and proposed to him that there seems no other visible remedy to interrupt or break his devotions, save making him eat tobacco by the hand of a Brahmin; and this proposal was made before the full Court of Ajmeer Shaw. And by the eating of which tobacco the Rishee became totally powerless of all the influence of "*Muntur*" and the daughter of Ajmeer Shaw joined herself in the calm of night in the same bed with the "Rishee;" but when the Rishee came to know that he was deceived by tobacco, secretly administered to him by Ajmeer Shaw, his pure soul left his body and he cursed, that the effect of the use of tobacco would prove injurious and bad just after his death. A supernatural voice was heard above, that the action of Cow, drove me from this world, and all the existing vices in this world would come to him who will hear and make others hear this (action of the Cow).

9 One who reads lessons on holidays becomes indigent; the days of his life are shortened, he suffers in both worlds. It is good to abstain from the bed of a woman who is in her courses and from the bed of a widow. A man should also abstain from having sexual intercourse with the following women viz:—

1 One who is not married.
2 One who dislikes veneral pleasures.
3 One descended from common ancestors.
4 One who is sick of any disease.

The remaining part of the water with which man cleans himself after privy, is impure.

The hand put in the mouth is impure. Dogs, Chundals, and the leavings of meal are impure. The water of a small pot is impure. These things which are impure according to Vedas and Poorans are not impure, for the persons who are mean and of adulterated castes, Baba Nanuk says that these things are fatal to animals (i. e. foolish men) but of worthy and good men. The Gooroo says, I have invented this religion for the sake of virtue, my seikhs should not enjoy the wealth given in charity and offered to gods. The covetous man who will not obey this order shall be made into a hog. One who worships Gooroo's feet day and night and behaves according to the customs of his family shall be saved from sins. A seikh should read this Sakhee and recite it for the benefit of others. Sakhee 88th finished.

SAKHEE EIGHTY-NINTH.

One day the Gooroo heard of the birth of his son Futteh Singh and said well has it been, the ocean of comfort has come into existence! after this he laughed and said, not this time but second time. The seikhs begged to have this explained to them. The Gooroo said, in his next birth this child shall be called by the name of Bhagwan * Singh and shall adopt the rules and practices of seikhism and shall be a ruler. In my presence he will rule and the Khalsa will obey his orders. I will also appear at that time and destroy Englishmen. One of my seikhs will marry an English wife. The religion of Muleches and the family of Toorks and Mahammedans will increase. The seikhism will also increase, but there shall be very little religious virtue in it. The ceremonies of Kaliyoga shall prevail, but no one will know it. When God granted me kingdom the Kuliyoga told me with folded hands, let your

* Maharaja Sher Shingh and Maharaja Duleep Singh and Raja Rundheer Singh Kapoor Sing.

reign be in my time, and I may live with your Punth.[1] You should protect me, as Juggan Nath has done in Juggan Nath territory, the Runchar god has done in Dawarka, the Vishonath has done in Kanshee, the Dhurm god in Koorchetur. I will do all your work, my and your reign will remain together in all the world. I (the Gooroo) told him what will you do? The Kuliyoga said, "I will glorify the name of God, I will produce quarrel between father and son, husband and wife. The people will leave their mothers and sisters and will be obedient to their wives. The father-in-law will have illicit intercourse with the son's wife, and the mother-in-law will enjoy veneral pleasures with her son-in-law. The slaves will enjoy the king's wives. The Brahmas will become covetous. The Shooders will be fed in religious ceremonies and the Brahmans will be driven out. No one will feel obliged for the favours done to him. Many irregularities shall prevail. The woman, who brings forth a son shall be respected, and one who brings forth a daughter shall be hated. The son will advise the father, and daughter-in-law will call her mother-in-law a liar. The pupils will inculcate religious precepts to their spiritual guides and will eat food with unclean hands. They will give up bathing, saying it does not suit their health. The people will always remain unhealthy and will eat more than the proper quantity. There shall be little love, but a great show of affection will be made to earn livelihood. The poets will adopt the subject of sexual pleasures for their compositions. Every house will make new worships every day. The Brahmans will sell Vedas, the Khutrees will sell lands, Bunyan's will sell houses and the Shooders will sell their children. The hungry and worthless fellows will become religious mendicants. Notwithstanding their wearing Julta,[2] deer's skin and wooden shoes they will

---

[1] The whole body of seikhs as the word "Church" denotes whole body of Christians.

[2] Long entagled hairs on the head of religious mendicants.

enjoy women, and will tell the public that a fortunate man obtains devotee's company. They will be hellish beings themselves and will lead others to hell. They will pay no attention to virtues. They will deceive the people by teaching religious precepts, bringing tears in their eyes and moving their heads as if it were in the love of God. They will be cheaters inside and will look fair outwardly. They will cause miscarriages of the widows. They will make the good women barren, by the effects of medicines. Where there will be much eagerness there will be much failure and the success will follow when it is not much cared for. The friends will become enemies and the enemies will become friends. Hearing this the Gooroo said, your feats are extraordinary O Kuliyoga, thy way will be like a juggler. My sungat will be the worshippers of the Name of God, you should assist them. Sakhee 89th finished.

SAKHEE NINETIETH.

The true Gooroo then said to the Kuliyoga, hear what I say and reply. My sungat are lovers of God and thy way is different. The Kuliyoga said, hear me, O Gooroo I tell thee from beginning, but do not reveal it. The[1] Gooroo related to me, this story O Sahib Singh and I now relate it to you. The Brahma knowing that Kuliyoga was desirous of making the Khalsa reign in his time, appointed Kuliyoga to exist at the time of Khalsa's reign. When Brahma found all the yogas proud, he said that your power will be according to the way you distribute justice, saying this the Brahma engaged himself in contemplations and remembered God. Each of the four yogas assumed the human forms and stood before the Brahma, who taught the first, Sutiyoga, political science

[1] This is the saying of Goor Bux Singh.

and asked him, how will you reign, O my son tell me here. The Sutiyoga said, I will bless or punish the whole country for one man's virtue or fault, the people will be engaged in devotions, truth, public feasts, worships &c., &c. The Brahmans will be devoted to religious duties as myself am a Brahm. The seed will bring forth fruit hundred times, the human age will be one lakh years. The Khut-ree will perform his military duties and will give charity.

The Bunyas will be engaged in trading. Thus all of the three castes will perform their respective duties. The Treta then said, O father, I am a Khutree, I will change the ancient customs, I will serve Brahman and cause public feasts to be given after the accumulation of wealth. I will cause the sins of the people to be obliterated. I will engage even the natives of paradise in performing good or bad actions. The seeds will bring forth fruit ten times. The human age will be ten thousand years. The people will fear from sins. I will be tenfold less than my elder brother, Sutiyoga, and will establish the path of virtue. The Dawaper then said, in my reign worship will be made in each house. The human age will be one thousand years. The seeds will bring forth fruit four times. The virtue and sins shall be cut in halves. The majority of Brahmans and Khutrees shall be engaged in trading and will not decide their cases themselves, but will apply for justice to the Rajahs. The Brahma then laughed and said, O Kuliyoga, thou art my youngest son, I love thee best, tell me your story as will be according to your will. The Kuliyoga laughed and with folded hands spoke humbly thus, I will bless or punish the very individuals for his virtues or sins. The human age will be one hundred years. The seeds will bring forth first only one time i. e. fields will be sown and reaped twice a year. A man shall have many children and his desires will be unbounded. Anything that strikes the mind will be carried out.

The Shooders will reign. The people will consider their own houses as sacred forests adapted to devotions. The name of God will be considered as effective as the verses of Veda. The sinners, men, and women, Brahmans and Shooders, persons of mean descent and children will be saved through the love of God. The Toorks will be born from mean women and the castes will be amalgamated. I will punish all without the name of God. The hell and paradise shall be under my rule, an epitome of which I will show on this earth. I will make the souls wander in 84,00,000 sorts of births. If you will ordain it this way, I will consent to go upon the earth. I will obey no other person except you. Sakhee 90th finished.

SAKHEE NINETY-FIRST.

The Brahma then said to the Kuliyoga, O my son, you are obedient to me, go upon the earth and establish the people in their duties and virtues; all the Munters[1] in your reign will become worthless and the Munter of the Name of God will only be the effective. In other yogas the people relied on devotions, Yogas[2] and worships, but in the Kuliyoga the repetition of the word Ram (God) will give success. O my son, in your reign I will prohibit all the gods to make interference. You will be at liberty to act as you like. You should be careful to maintain the blessings of God's name. Your reign will be a good one, your words will be true and a little devotion will impart much blessings. You should remember to give up three things, viz, appropriating another man's property, enjoying the woman who is not married and neglect from remembering the name of God every moment. You should sing the songs of God, remember God, love God, believe in God and trust completely in God. A man should

---

[1] Incantations.

[2] Public feasts.

also remember God at the point of death, for he will be saved this way. If he thus worships God, he will be able to swim across the ocean of the world. You should fear a person who gives himself up to God. This is my habit, so I teach you also this. You should rely in no other thing except the Name of God, through the effects of which human soul is able to form through three worlds and to obtain salvation. One who enjoys his own wife only, speaks the truth and lives upon whatever he finds, is the true devotee. After this the Brahma said, Sutiyoga will remain in my head, the Treta in my arms, the Dawaper in my legs and thou Kuliyoga will be the slave of my feet. In the Veda it is written that each man will obtain salvation in his own caste, this is the truth you should remember it. You all the yogas after enjoying your respective reigns, you should come and be absorbed in my limbs. All this is written in a Sanskrit Book called "Brahm Sungata" There are four sorts of words, viz., Para, Pasantee, Madbia and Baikhree, and the Narain, Nar, Soorustee and Byas Deva are their respective gods. A man should shut his breath in the Naval towards the right side and absorb his attention in the God. This is the Naval worship taught by the Gooroo to Muthra Missur. Saying this, O Sahib Singh, the Kuliyoga went away, I have related to you this Sakhee. Whoever will read or hear it will be happy. Sakhee 91st finished.

SAKHEE NINETY-SECOND.

Once the Gooroo was sitting with pleasure in the assembly of his seikhs, who asked him about the virtuous practices, which a man should daily perform. The Gooroo laughed and the seikhs were ashamed. The Gooroo then repeated what Gooroo Arjun had spoken in the answer of a similar question and praised, "Sookhmunee" [1] and Jupjee. [2]

---

[1] and [2] Sacred treatise of the Seikhs in the Grunth Sahib.

Once in Gooroo Arjun's Durbar Pindee Lall and Nund Lall asked a question, when one Nund Singh addressed the Gooroo Arjun to remove all doubts, say O true king, I have seen a great wonder, which was that an evil spirit of a demon effected a seikh in the Sarai. While this conversation was going on, the following persons arrived there viz., Birj Lall Pandah, Nihal Chund, Man Chand, Sookhdeva Pundit, Mandass Bairagee, Mudden Gir Sunyasee, Alum, Fukeer Hosian Ali Syad, Birkha, Sookha, Goonia, Goonna, and other Gooroo Arjun's friends and bowed before the Gooroo. After this Bhai Suddoo and Muddoo musicians began to sing sacred songs. At that time Gooroo Arjun replied, O Bhai Nund Singh, that seikh, who is effected by evil spirit in the Sarai, was not perhaps in the habit of reading Jupjee. The Seikhs then asked, whether Jupjee protects the body or gives the salvation. The Gooroo replied that it gives both salvation and protection. upon this Brij Lall Panda said, O true king, hear my word also. I one day saw Baba Nanuk in a dream and heard the praise of Jupjee at that time, I repeat to you that verse. The Gooroo Arjun said, recite O Brother, you are the loving Pundit of Gooroo's family. Pundit Birj Lall then blessed the Gooroo Arjun and read the following verse of Sanskrit, whose translation is, O Gooroo destroy the enemies who trouble me day and night in my house, and protect me and show me yourself in the dream, reciting this verse Pundit Birj Lall said that he saw Gooroo Nanuk and Gooroo Arjun in the dream, who taught me the following verse, viz., In the age of Kuliyoga a person should repeat the words, "Oong Sut Nam" (God the true Name) in the beginning of the following enterprises, viz., obtaining salvation, starting, obtaining wealth or knowledge or arts, performing virtuous acts, retiring from the world, worshiping gods, going to women, employing a servant, trying to obtain a son collecting wealth, in diseases, subjecting the mind, fighting, going to a stranger's house following virtuous ways and giving heavy charity.

Boodha Sahib then said, O Sahib Singh, the Panda (Birj Lall) after reciting the above verse, asked the meaning of it from Gooroo Arjun, who replied, O Bhai Birj Lall this verse is on the subject of Jupjee, the "Munter[1] of the mind." A man should read the five letters "Oom Sut Nam," for this destroys the effects of Rheumatism, Cough and Bile, gives salvation, destroys calamity, and if it be read after the meals, it exalts man's position, digests the food and saves from dying. These five letters should be repeated ten thousand times for obtaining wealth, virtue, god's pleasure, women, sons, success in quarrel, to get rid of the dismal state of mind and to charm another man's heart. This should be done with full belief and with paying obeisance to the Gooroo. A seikh should give 10th part of his earnings in charity. These five words should also be read in walking in collecting any thing, in taking and giving charity, at the time when a man's disposition is changed or when he has been looked at with evil eyes of a ghost or a witch. These are the meanings of the above verse which Gooroo Arjun taught to Birj Lall Panda in the dream. After this Gooroo Gobind Singh explained the meanings of the verse, and said that a person in order to obtain success in the before said enterprises should repeat the beginning letters of Jupjee, 200 times, 25,000 times, 36,000 times, 38,000 times, 1,00,000 times and 1,50,000 times viz., as many thousand times as he takes the letters of the beginning of Jupjee. After this repetition of the verse, a man should make Hom[2] of the same verse. By doing this a man obtains success and his hands are broken, by the favour of the magnificent faced Gooroo. One who is learned in Veda, should repeat the verse half the number of times

[1] Incantation.

[2] Casting in the fire by reading sacred verses.

as a foolish man. The Khutree should repeat thrice as much as the first and the "Shooders" four times as much as the first. The Bunya should read $3\frac{1}{2}$ times as much as the first and the rest as much as written above. A virtuous seikh of the Gooroo should repeat the whole verse from the word "Oom" to the words "Gooroo Pershad" for salvation. In order to obtain true knowledge, yoga science, purification of mind, and collection of wealth, a man should repeat 5 words. After reading the verse and making Hom as above said, he should make the "Marjun"[1] with the repetition of the names of God as mentioned in the following verse, viz. We pay obeisance to the God, who is represented by the sacred word "Oom," who is the truth, the connoisseur the source of creation, the shape of Yaj[2] the creator, the Protector, the Saviour, the best of all, the Golden, the sky, the One beyond worldly delusions, the Round, the End of the world, the well-praised, the Eternity, the Unborn, the Heaven, the Omnipresent, the Imperishable, the death, the Husband of Luchhmee godess, the word "Image" the Husband of Ruma godess, the Lord of the three worlds, the Durable, the Master of the Universe the Figureless, the Owner of the house, the Beginning of letters, the Breaker, and the sacred word "Oonkar." A man while reading the above names should cast sweetmeat in the fire with the repetition of the word "Swaha," but he should recollect the two letters "Juppa" in his mind at the same time. He should then make adoration for his own comfort. After the words "Goor Purshad" he should repeat 36 letters and 50 letters and the name of 5 elements, viz., earth, water, fire, air and sky. He should read 8 letters and 5 letters in heart when he begins to write anything. Generally he should read 25 and 36 letters in all works and 38 letters at the time of beginning to learn sciences

[1] Sprinkling water on one's own body after the hom ceremony.

[2] Sacred ceremony of giving public feast.

and arts After this the Gooroo said, O Bhai Birj Lall, you are a Brahman of excellent family, consider deeply the religious duties of Kuliyoga age and the sections of Jupjee. Whoever being a Khutree will make this Hôm for 1,00,000 times, he shall be saved, for through the effect of Jupjee mind is purified, the sprinkling of water over which Jupjee is read, purifies the way. One who is in want of anything or wishes to please or to subject a Devta, or is travelling in a foreigin country, or is going to use a good medicine, he should read 2nd section of the Jupjee, viz., the words "Ad such" and in the days of calamity and loss, 3rd section of the same, viz., "Gave Kotan Mudh" should be read. When a man wants to succeed in a difficult enterprise, he should pay presents to the Gooroo. He should read 4th section at the time of building a new house and learning a new science and repeat the word "Jup" seven times. In short each section of "Jupjee" should be read for special purposes as detailed below.

In smart Enterprises, ... 5th Sec.
In Battle and War, ... 6th ,,
For the release of Prisoner and a pregnant woman ... ... 7th and 8th ,,
In Conspiracy, ... 9th ,,
Subjecting a Devta to one's own will, ... 10th ,,
In dealing in Horses and Conveyances, ... 11th ,,
To escape from expected evil, ... 12th ,,
To obtain "Sidhees" and success in Government affairs, ... 13th ,,
To write a "Junter" ... ... 14th ,,
To get rid of the effect of a ghost, 15th ,,

To be saved from a Dain[1] ... ... 16th Sec.

To get a delicious food, ... 17th " read 18 days.

To acquire Knowledge quickly, ... 18th "

To be strong in Brain, ... 19th "

To be married, ... 20th "

To obtain children, ... 21st

To remedy the repeatedly dying of one's children, one after another, ... 22nd "

To kill enemies, ... 23rd "

To be the friend of a wise man, 24th "

To acquire beauty and honor and to captivate the mind, ... 25th "

To deceive, ... 26th "

To acquire bodly power, ... 27th "

To be saved from the effects of a heinous offence, ... 28th

To remedy the effects of poison, ... 29th "

To increase the milk of a cow, ... 30th "

To be cured from 3rd day fever ... 31, 32 & 33 Sec.

To be cured from daily fever, ... 34th "

Each of these sections should be read 40 times.

The obtain success in any enterprize. The whole of Jupjee 10 times.

To obtain a wish. The whole of Jupjee 20 times.

To obtain Kingdom. The whole of Jupjee 30 times.

To obtain salvation. The whole of Jupjee 40 times.

To obtain a footing in Society, ... 35th Sec.

To conquer a fort,... ... ... 36th "

For bravery, ... 37th "

---

[1] A woman who eats the heart of human beings.

To visit a devotee or a Rajah, ... 38th Sec.
To become like an angel, ... 39th "
To become like four-handed god,
Vishnoo," ... ... 40th "

If the whole of "Jupjee" be read 4 times, be written 4 times and fire sacrifice according to the prescribed form be made by reading four times, then the man so doing obtains everlasting life. A man should read the verses in which the praise of "Jupjee" is contained and should love the Gooroo for the devotions of those persons, who have their faith in, and love to the Gooroo are acceptable by God. After relating so far Pundit Birj Lall said, that he had heard this praise of "Jupjee" from those persons who knew it from Gooroo Arjun and Baba Nanuk and that he has now related it for the benefit of the devotees. This, he said, should not be made known to the wicked and ill-minded persons, for they shall become faithless by hearing it and shall give up to serve the devotees and Brahmans. A good man should leave the following things altogether, viz , envy, pride and hypocricy and should believe in the Gooroo's words as well as in Veda's precepts. By reading "Jupjee" millions of sins are destroyed and giving charity every day increases the wisdom and the wealth of a man and produces desire of performing good actions, in him. To captivate a Devta by the effects of "Munters" enables a man to obtain success, to get rid from his natural stupidity and to increase wealth. A woman is also saved by so doing from her evils, but it is sin to recite these things to a person, who does not feel interest in it. If a person will read Jupjee according to the manner prescribed by the Gooroo, he will surely obtain success and all luxuries of this world. A man becomes "Sidh" and obtains Gooroos' pleasure by giving presents to the Gooroo. Baba Nanuk has most kindly revealed this method for his followers and Gooroo Arjun has made its meaning known to the public. They had these things told them by God in a dream and I have written the same here for the benefit of the seikhs. The God becomes kind to him, who sees, peruses, recites, teaches or praises the Jupjee, for this is a collection of words which flowed from the sacred mouth of Gooroo Arjun. In the age of Kuliyoga the people of 4 castes should be taught four sorts of worship, for there are four sorts of sounds, viz., Para, Pasantee, Madhman and Vaikhree related by the "Vedas." These four sounds have four special places of their utterance, viz., navel, mind, throat and tongue respectively. It is useful to read by these four voices and this is the real value of reading. Through the effects of repeating Jupjee spiritually the well-behaved and respectable Pundit Birj Lall enjoyed divine pleasures in the presence of Gooroo Arjun and his friends, Nund Lall, Pindee Lall, Khan Chund, Bidhee Chund, Alum Shah, Mandass and Sookh Mudden gladly accepted what Gooroo Arjun had told him (Pundit Birj Lall) in a dream, when his mind did fly like a bird to him (Gooroo Arjun). At that time Gooroo Arjun had thrice told Pundit Birj Lall that Jupjee is a precious jewel and that he had been able to see Gooroo's beautiful face through the effects of reading "Jupjee" and that after his death Pundit Birj Lall shall now obtain salvation. The drinking of water over which the words, "Oong Sutgoor Purshad Kurta Poorkh" are read, prolongs the life, cures all bodily diseases and is useful for charming the heart of a woman, if read at midnight. The devotee shall be able to obtain enjoyment and pleasure by this practice.

These things have been related by Kesho Brahman by the implied orders of the Gooroo. Having heard these things from Gooroo Arjun, the people enjoyed the rest of paradise and all their troubles were removed. Now hear, O Brother, whoever will read "Jupjee" the grace of the Gooroo shall always remain with him and he shall go to live in the presence of God. Whoever being a seikh will read this sacred treatise he shall obtain the dignity of a "Vedantee" and God shall attend him as He attended Dhunna Devotee's Cows. Sakhee 92nd finished.

SAKHEE NINETY-THIRD.

In the Sub: 1730 the real object of "Jupjee" was known. This is straight road built for the seikhs, who if they will read, write or hear it with love, should obtain success and worldly pleasures and being escaped from all troubles shall be able to swim across the ocean of the world .This treatise should be read from Gooroo, to whom some present should be made and then its daily repetition will shower blessings on the reader. The 10th Gooroo has ordered that the following verse which means, "In the beginning is Truth, the next is Truth, O Nanuk, there is truth and shall be truth," is the best of all and the Gooroo in his last moments' repeated these sacred words and exclaimed I am also repeating the "Munter" of the Gooroo. O friends the true Gooroo assumed the body of man and has shown us his miraculous feats throughout the life. On one occasion the Gooroo predicted that an age shall come when the people shall become fond of witchcrafts and magics ; every house shall pretend to know and perform several sorts of magical wonders. My seikhs in those days should not pay attention to these things, but should engage themselves in divine worship and devotions. A man can obtain strength and goodness of conduct according to the faith he has in his Gooroo, therefore, he should remember God, who can grant salvation to him by repeating the word, "Wah Gooroo," all desires are obtained and every enterprise of the reader proves successful.

O seikhs, apply yourselves to worship with love to the Gooroo, for the name of God will give success to all your works. Once in a great battle the Gooroo's horse stopped suddenly from proceeding further, whereupon the Gooroo ordered his groom, Buden Singh, to search the grass; it was done so and a leaf of tobacco was found in it. The Gooroo cautioned the groom for future to search the grass before he gives it to the horse and ordered that none of his seikhs of "Pahool" ceremony should ever smoke tobacco, which was sown by the Mahammedans and which destroyed the Hindooism of devotees. Those who are sinners do not believe in the Gooroo's words. The very field in which the tobacco is sown is impure. Sakhee 93rd finished.

SAKHEE NINETY-FOURTH.

After that, on the next day when the Gooroo was crowded with a large body of his followers, two Mooltanee seikhs came and stood before him with folded hands and asked him about the bad results of smoking tobacco, saying that they were the descendants of Sungat Khutree of Pahree caste and had left their native city, Mooltan, for the purpose of asking this question. The Gooroo replied, O brothers, believe in my word, I will relate to you what "Shivajee" had foretold in the "Asgundh Puran." Once "Sham Kartic" addressed Shivajee, saying O father tell us what is vicious in this fatal world and what sort of people will live in the "Kuliyoga" age, tell us what have the devotees related about this. The Shevajee being moved with paternal love said that the repetition of "sin-destroying Munter" purifies the mind and the bathing in the river Ganges clears the body from uncleanness, but both these things become spoiled by touching tobacco. By eating it the fruit of all virtuous and devotional acts are annihilated, and by smoking, Munters become unholy. The land in which the tobacco is once sown becomes unholy like the lands of "Mugdh" Desh and remains so till one year. Tobacco had no existence in Sutyoga, Treta and Dawaper ages, it sprung out in the age of Kuliyoga only. There was a king in the descendants of Pandavs, named "Nem Nath" who treated his subjects with injustice and tyranny. The people being reduced to utmost straitness fled to a "Peer" in the eastern country, who introduced them to the king of "Boorgan" where the force of unholy men prevailed. This king sent his son "Ajmeer" to assist the pressed people, and to re-settle them in their own country. This prince marched with the army against the tyrant king, "Nem Nath," and conquering him established his own rule in the country. After some time, Ajmeer Shah in order to see a retired devotee went to Pobkur country and reached near a temple situated in a forest of Palm trees. Here he met a shepherd, who guided him to the retired devotee. Ajmeer Shah requested the devotee to worship the Shivajee with water and "Bill" tree leaves on his behalf. The devotee did so and through the effect of this a supernatural person appeared and ordered Ajmeer Shah to ask something from him. Ajmeer Shah told him that he wished his kingdom to be established and rooted firm in the newly conquered country, for he was afraid that the Hindoos would not allow him to reign long in the territories once acquired by him by the force of arms. The person directed him to go to another devotee stationed at a place little further from that situation. Ajmeer Shah proceeded further to that devotee, who told him that his object will be gained from the medicine of cow's sacrifice. Ajmeer Shah asked him where he could find that medicine. The devotee told him that in the west there was a place, where cow's sacrifice was made and the cow was not again made alive. The place consequently became impure and a plant sprung up from there, the leaves of which have the effect of improving the power of "Toorks" and of multiplying them. There once lived a king named "Ajapal," whose beautiful daughter had also succeeded in enticing away a devotee's son by means of tobaccq leaves, she being taught by Soomoond Rishee to use this plan. In that place of cow's sacrifice the leaves of sin (i. e. tobacco) sprung up and consequently have the effect of annihilating all the fruits of virtue, religious devotions and pilgrimages. So Ajmeer Shah brought the tobacco leaves and spread them in the country of Hindoos. This is the fruit of Koliyoga and is worse than even garlic plant. Since the day the seed of tobacco was sown, the Devtas left to descend from heavens upon earth. This story was also related by Keshiv Missur, who testified to its being true. O my friends, I after full enquiry have given up to smoke tobacco and have repeated this story before you that you may also follow my example. This Sakheo has the effect of annihilating evil. Sakhee 94th finished.

SAKHEE NINETY-FIFTH.

O seikhs, if you wish to obtain salvation, you better give up the smoking of tobacco altogether. It is better to die than to eat the leavings of another man's food. If even a little of tobacco be eaten or smoked, it causes the angels and the deceased ancestors to fly from the person, who used it. The water touched by the person, who smokes tobacco is as bad as wine. The wine sends seven generations of the man who uses it, to hell, the "Bhung" consumes only the body of its user, but one who eats the eaving of what has been eaten by the world, *his* 100 generations are burnt. The backbiting burns the innumerable generations. In the age of Kuliyoga, whoever gives up to smoke tobacco, obtains salvation, is accepted by God, his hopes are fulfilled, and his devotions become fruitful. The Shaster calls the tobacco as not worthy of eating, the wine as not worthy of drinking and the backbiting as meanness and foolishness in a man. The following persons should be considered as descended from ass.

1 One who being a Khutree rides on a pregnant mare.

2 One who being a Brahman rides on a Bull.

3 One who being a "Sunyassee" rides on a horse.

4 The woman who plays in the company of men.

5 One who being a wise man envies anothers fortune.

6 One who being a Shooder rebels against a Brahman.

7 One who being a king takes bribe.

8 One who being a devotee does not like the praise and fortune of another.

9 One who contracts friendship with virgin Girls.

10 One who being an old man is debaucherous.

11 One who sells his daughter in marriage.

Such persons in their next birth shall become bulls, Eunuchs and cripples. Cursed be the life of that man, who loads a cow with burden, steals the clothes of another man, eats the leavings of another man's food, deprives persons from the means of their livelihood, and causes enmity between two friends. Such persons cannot obtain heaven at any time. Those who leave their faith and act against the Gooroo's precepts, have innumerable sins attached to them. Those devotees who perform 10 sorts of virtues with their tongues, bodies and hearts, do not go to "Yum's" regions. This my saying is true. Baba Nanuk has secretly taught the following precepts, viz.

To abstain from killing animals.

To abstain from coveting a stranger's wife and proprety.

To abstain from wishing ill to others.

To abstain from addressing others with obscene words.

To abstain from thinking of women not legally married.

To abstain from praising a bad man.

To abstain from following the bad examples of an enemy.

To forgive the first fault of foolish persons.

My seikh should follow these ways and one who is humble in heart and strong in his faith is always joined with me. All sins spring up from desire, which upsets all virtues. It is not good to flatter a rich person, to become a constant flatterer, to chatter too much. A friend who is in the habit of joking is also bad. One who leaves God, but applies himself to arms, I take care not to let him fall. A seikh should not allow Mahammedans to be acquainted with the secrets of his heart and should not swear by the Gooroo. Sakhee 95th finished.

SAKHEE NINTY-SIXTH.

Once a body of seikhs asked the Gooroo, whether the present usage of shaving and cutting short the hairs of the head and body as taught and preached by the devotees and Brahmans of the present age was their own invention, for they said, the devotees and Brahmans of the ancient age used to wear long hairs on their head. The Gooroo spoke to Nund Rai, saying that since the time the well known Brahman heroe called "Paras Ram" annihilated the Khutrees, the Brahmans entertained envious feelings with them and reducing them to subjection ordered them to keep their heads shaved as a punishment for them. Believe this word of mine to be true. The Brahmans having acquired power filled tanks with Khutree's blood, caused the half head of the Mahammedans to be shaved and called them "Trimoondee," i e. shaved in three places. They established their own Police and reduced the Shooders to poverty. They forcibly deprived Shooder Rajahs from their wealth and becoming proud forgot the true God altogether. The Shooders being afraid of oath delivered all their Books to Bhrahmans; for in those days the keeping of Books for Shooders was as great an offence as stealing, cheating &c. and was punishable with imprisonment and death. In short those who being afraid submitted to them, became their followers; there is no use in continuing this story any further. Those who apply themselves closely to devotions, cross the river of the miseries of this world, and those who are engaged in empty talks are drowned. The devotions and love of God are to be praised. All men are sinners. All persons are sinners and there are numerous troubles in the religious law. As long as the material body exists, the religious Law can be acted upon, but when the spirit exists in a state of dream, what actions can be performed? What good actions did Brahma perform that he was appointed the law giver of the angels. The good actions inculcated by the "Vedas" for the persons of all castes and positions are Devotions, repeating God's name by rosary, giving cash to Brahmans, going on pilgrimage, giving charity, fasting and austerities. The mind is known by mind, the senses by senses and the wisdom by wisdom. Even a foolish man can understand the difference between God and the gods, O Sahib Singh, believe that I have enmity with no body, be acquainted with your own beauty, this is the result of my "Durshun." Hear the stories of South. Besides these the Gooroo related 500 Sakhees and distributed them according to the following order, viz.

To Ram Kour, Goor Bux Singh, ... 100
To Kabli Mull, ... 100
To Mooltanee Seikhs, ... 100
To Raitee Poorbia, ... 100
To Soorut Singh of Agra, ... 100

The Gooroo assumed his residence in Dukkun and at last died there. Sakhee 96th finished.

SAKHEE NINTY-SEVENTH.

Once when the Gooroo was travelling, with his followers, to Dukkun, he arrived at the door of Dadoo devotee and with his bow saluted the house of Dadoo. The followers were astonished to see this and laughed (This Sakhee was recited to me by the Sidh of Hurria Husna, who had also given me a handkerchief saying, O Bhai, Ram Kour, this handkerchief was given to you by the Gooroo). The seikhs then begged the Gooroo to explain this mystery to them, saying, that he always ordered them not to worship the graves and the "Mussanee" goddess, but that he himself has, this day, bowed his head before the grave of Dadoo. The Gooroo smiled and said that he had done so in order to pay fine to the Khalsa, for the Khalsa is Gooroo's and the Gooroo of Khalsa. Saying this the Gooroo paid 500 Rs. to the Khalsa and said, that he pays this as a fine to the Khalsa; likewise every other seikh sinning against the Khalsa should pay fine to the Khalsa, but if he would not do so, his treasures should be reduced to ashes. Once Bahadur Shah, the Emperor, hearing of this fact asked the Gooroo about this, saying that the religion of the Hindoos is raw for they worship the pictures drawn by themselves on walls, give water and food to their deceased ancestors and cast the purified butter into the fire. The Gooroo replied that all the acts of the Hindoos are excellent, for by labouring and serving, the field yields fruit to the cultivator, the cow gives milk, the kings give money and the master pays his servant. Whatever way is followed, the same gives fruit to its follower. The Brahma, whose picture is worshipped created two sorts of men, viz. "Astuk" and "Nastuk" The former are the Hindoos and the latter Mahammedans. So the mental desire of you, the Mahammedans creates diseases and the Hindoos are healty creatures. Those who are sick, eat and drink idolly and the healthy Hindoos serve and eat. Whoever nourishes the seed gets the fruit of it. Likewise Brahmans and Hindoos reap the fruit of their worship in heaven. The faith of you the Mahammedans is more raw, for you worship graves ; do they not give you what you desire ? Your own saying will be falsified by the answer. In our religion there is only one God who neither does nor causes to be done, but still he exists for ever and ever and protects him, who labors for him. You being a slave worship your God. Have you ever heard or seen that God ? One who has no form or sign is called "Akall," whom then doth thou pay your obeisance and salutations ? Why doth thou undergo the trouble of bending your head before Mecca. Your saying is no more than empty ambition. O Emperor, this my word is complete and full. The Mahammedans worship their Peers and prophets and the Hindoos worship three times in a day. They both are wrong, therefore I have relinquished them both and have established my third religion, that of Khalsa. There is only one God, the imperishable and the Omnipresent and his worship is excellent for the old and young Khalsa, who have given up the worship of graves and gods and leaving idolatory altogether have fixed their sight on the ultimate object. O Emperor thy father is imprisioned in the above regions and you have taken possession of his Empire ; you dont send him money for his expenses nor become sorry for him. Your father has nothing to expend while I have got treasures hoarded up, for me, there. Your father is weeping and crying in higher regions and is extremely poor. One who is poor, either becomes a slave or a thief and robber. When such things were considered and written by the Gooroo to the Emperor, he was humbled and was convinced of the miraculous powers of the Gooroo, whom he addressed in humble terms, saying, O Peer, accept the salutation of kissing your feet from me, for I have determined to be your servant. Sakhee 97th finished.

SAKHEE NINTY-EIGHTH.

One day the grandson of Painde Khan Puthan came and saluted the Gooroo in Durbar. The Gooroo finding him a handsome youth without beard asked him of his caste, name and parentage and of the reasons of his coming there. The boy replied that he was the son of Saide Khan, the grandson of Painde Khan and the great grandson of "Gool Khat" and that his mother considering the Gooroo as prophet had sent him there and that he was much pleased to see the magnificent face of the Gooroo. The Gooroo paid 5 gold mohurs to him and ordered him to come every day to the Gooroo's house and to play with him at chess &c. Hearing this, the boy was pleased in heart and paying obeisance to the Gooroo went home. Since that day the boy made his practice to come to the Gooroo every day and received 5 Rs. per diem. Seeing this, seikhs one day asked the Gooroo of the reason of his so much loving the Mahammedan boy, adding that it was contrary to his precepts; as he always used to advise the Khalsa to be at enmity with the Mahammedans. The Gooroo said there was secret concealed in this and that they themselves will know about it after few days. That he well remembered his grandfather, Painde Khan and the bloody battle that was fought with him. That he pitied the young boy, who appears a good nice youth to him. After this one day two seikhs of "Nepal" came before the Gooroo and presented him with two very sharp excellent daggers, after which they returned to their residence. The Gooroo when playing at "dice-cloth" with the Mahammedan boy, used to tell him that a worthy son should revenge his father, no matter whether he be the servant of his enemy or not. The boy had once mentioned this to his mother, who had dissuaded him from ever venturing to do so. The Gooroo on this occasion after playing at Dice-cloth with the boy, laid himself down on bed, made the boy sit near him, gave the dagger in his hand and repeating the words, "cursed is the life of that man and woe to his position, who finding his fathers enemy alone does not revenge his murdered father," allowed the Mahammedan youth by signs to kill him. The young boy inflicted three wounds upon the breast of the Gooroo, who then being enraged exclaimed, "the Puthans have attacked me." Hearing this one "Lukha Singh" seikh ran and cutting off the boy's head attended to take care of the Gooroo. The Gooroo then advised his seikhs never to trust Mahammedans and every Hindoo or Mahammedan, who heard this accident cursed the Puthan boy. Bahadur Shah, the Emperor of Dehlie hearing this, sent very skillful doctors to treat the Gooroo. These doctors cured the Gooroo's wounds and after remaining there for 15 days took leave of the Gooroo and returned to their house in Dehlie. The Gooroo then bathed after recovery, the bands of joy were played, the seikhs were filled with pleasure and the houses were illuminated. The Gooroo then ordered a canopy and the wall of a tent to be pitched up and prohibited all persons to go to that place except the prescribed time. One day a person with a torch in his hand descended from heaven and falling upon the Gooroo's feet delivered him a letter, which no one could know in what letters and language it was written. After the Gooroo had read the letter the messenger disappeared like the air and returned to heaven. After that, on the 2nd of the lunar month, two messengers of the god of death came to the Gooroo and delivering him two bows returned to their regions. The Gooroo drew those bows and his wounds were torn. The seikhs asked of the reason of this and were told that he (the Gooroo) is suffering the results of his own good or bad actions, that they should make preparations for his departure and that he had received message from heaven and was ready to leave the world for taking his residence there. In order to besiege the Mahammedans the Gooroo recollected Baba Nanuk in his heart and such was the order of Baba Nanuk in the letter, which was read by Sahib Sing and Dan Sing, the seikhs, and which the Gooroo put upon his head for 5 hours as a sign of respect. The Gooroo then advised the seikhs to keep the letter without reading it and to burn it at the time of the arrival of the angels. The Gooroo after speaking to all, felt pain and through the yoga practises, keeping up his breath on the 3rd and 4th of the lunar month breathed his last on the 5th of the same. The Hindoos and Mahammedans began to say among themselves that on account of the knowledge of "Vedant" both worlds were alike for the Gooroo. Sakhee 98th finished.

SAKHEE NINTY-NINTH.

In the morning the door was crowded with the seikhs and all the Hindoos and Mahammedans, the pacifiers of the Gooroo's limbs were collected and expressed their love to the Gooroo. When the Gooroo was at the point of death, he caused "Koosha" grass and the seeds of Sesamum to be spread under his bed and taking a sword in his hands sat down upon the bed and read five verses which meant that God's lovers and the God are the same and that as a bubble rises up and again perishes in the river so a man springs up and resinks in the Godhead. At such a time the Gooroo appeared to every one but could not be touched. This was astonishing to all. The Gooroo then girded his lions, fastened a dagger to his girdle, took up a knife, a javelin, a bow and arrows. Being thus well armed he contracted the limbs of his body and fixing has attention in the forehead left his body of elements as a serpent leaves his slough. A loud voice was raised in the heaven and residents of paradise cried out, Hail! Hail! Hail! The residents of the earth raised their cries and then took the holy corpse to be burnt. The funeral file was prepared and a large quantity of sandal wood, "Agar,"[1] purified butter &c., being put therein, the corpse, which had been wrapped in precious magnificent clothes was burnt in it. The ashes were afterwards searched and nothing found in it except a small knife. The Brown Horse of the Gooroo also disappeared so the people thought that the Gooroo took his horse with him.

After that all the seikhs, Sadhees and Pundits removed to "Alwer Kot" and thence went on to "Gyajee," where they performed the funeral obsequies of the Gooroo, whose body was thus purified.

I have heard this Sakhee five times from the mouth of the Seikhs. At one time an Oodassee Fakeer of Hussun saw me and began to call me, one year after that my mind was filled with doubts, when the Gooroo showed his blessed face to me and ordered me to commit these Sakhees to writing very carefully. O Sahib Singh, hear what I say and see my shadow in the morning. The Gooroo then fulfilled what he had said in dream. He had told me in the same dream that when Ahmad Shah shall come, he will call us and at that time after obtaining the

[1] The name of a sweet smelling wood in India.

Gooroo's Durshun, we will get the fruit of our services, and O Brother there is an end to every thing in this world Ram, Krishen, Bishen, Shunker and all the other Gods and the 10 Gooroos did at last leave this world. These 99 Sakhees have been related for the Gooroo's seikhs. One Sakhee has been reserved for Nainee seikh, who shall be our pupil in Dhurm Kot. In order to confirm his faith the Gooroo had given his Durshun to him.

Whoever will read or hear these Sakhees with love and will contemplate upon them carefully, the Gooroo will grant him food and salvation and his desires shall be obtained. The Ram, the Gooroo, the services, and those who read or hear these Sakhees are true. Sakhee 99th finished.

SAKHEE ONE-HUNDREDTH.

The Boodha Sahib then said that the Gooroo in his presence wrote the following order to Sahib Singh: "O Sahib Singh, you should write the accounts of death as related by Bhai Ram Kour in the presence of Nainee, and keep it." At that time I was not present personally, but the Gooroo had told me all this in a dream. After this the King Ahmad Shah came from Kabool and other people had come with him for inspecting the country of India. They had put up in Dhurm Kot town. Nainee had seen all this with his own eyes and I hearing from him have written it accordingly fixing my mind in the feet of the Gooroo. The people of Dhurm Kot felt terrified from the invader Ahmad Shah, and their faces became red with fear. They left Dhurm Kot and in good time arrived at Rampoor. The Gooroo was attended at that time by Nainee seikh, who fell upon the Gooroo's feet and said O great king fulfil my desires. The Gooroo was put to ease and comfort by the services of Nainee, who served the Gooroo zealously for one year and obtained what was promised to him. Nainee was once imprisoned at Lahore by the king of Jummoo and he at the time had prayed to the Gooroo and was released. The Gooroo remained for $2\frac{1}{2}$ years with him after that time and taught him many good ways of worship. They both (the Gooroo and Nainee) once went to see Mitha Peer, who finding that the Gooroo was true guide asked him of the rules and methods of worshiping God. The Gooroo at the time related the rules and practices, of yoga science, by the effect of which desires are annihilated and the true knowledge of God is obtained and all the superstitions of the mind easily vanish. At that time Nainee who was present there asked about the comfort-giving Sakhee of Gooroo Gobind Singh, and Ram Kour told him that the king of Jummoo will serve Runjeeta * and his father will give up his life for the sake of name. He was the daughter's son of the Chief of Kuloor and had met the Gooroo at Anundpoor. The Gooroo having a knowledge of future success called him his own and he remained for seven years with the Gooroo, who at last granted him a sword a dagger, a javelin, a gun, Lahoree bow, and other arms ; he having taken these fell upon the Gooroo's feet and asked how he should behave in future. The Gooroo told him that he was well up, in arms and that he will obtain success in difficulties. The Gooroo further addressed him as follows, I will give you "Durshun," you should pay respect to my arms and believe that I will shortly come to your family.* There is no difference between you and me. O Nainee you will see with your own eyes that your service, shall bear fruit in Jummoo. After this the King of Noorpoor ordered his men to kill the "Kutch" family when one Goordass took up his javelin and opposed them at the head of Kutoches, who prepared Karah Prashad for the Gooroo every day and uttered the words "Wah-

* Maharaja Ranjit Singh of Lahore.

* Family Paharia Rajas.

gooroo ke Futteh" from their mouths. The Rajah then asked one person named Ruttun as to how he was able to see the deceased Gooroo and in order to try this took that person to his palace. In the morning he prepared for worship, caused Karah Prashad to be made and gave it to the Rajah, who ate it with great taste and pleasure. The ashes were then ordered to be spread in the plains and Rutten repeating the name of the Gooroo, rose up and said to Rajah, Behold horsemen are standing outside and are calling me to accompany them to the forests for gaming. The Rajah considering him a mad man remained silent only uttering the word Han," but the Vazeer denied to go out. After some time when they saw the marks of horse's hoofs in the plains, they were astonished. Rutten Deva on that day went out to hunt and when returning he went to his bed, he saw the beautiful face of the Gooroo in a dream and began to worship the Gooroo from that day. This beautiful Sakhee was related to us by Nainee seikh himself. The remaining part of this Sakhee is to be related by Narain Missur, whom the Gooroo appointed for the purpose and then making preparations for departure assumed silence, and fixing his attention within himself left this body and went to heavens. O Sahib Singh, here my word, Missur Narain shall meet us in Koora Mull's house in Jummoo being effected by the love of the Gooroo. We have seen with our own eyes what he told us and what we had heard from our ancestors. Rutten Deva has seen these things with his own eyes, let us go to him and ask him about the Gooroo's death. The Nainee then with the present of a Rupee and Narain Missur taking cardamums with him met Rutten Deva. They all three were filled with sacred love as well as all other persons created by God. They remained engaged in Sacred discourses for one month and the place was filled with happiness as the " Mydh" country with the waters of Googees. Rutten Deva said I reveal you secret things, the Gooroo took me in his lap and told me that a time shall come when he and we shall make a job together and shall see each other. We then took leave and came to our houses. Thus we also obtained this Sakhee. O Sahib Singh, write and keep it, this is a present for the Seikhs, who feel anxious to hear it. This Sakhee of the last days of the Gooroo has been written after full enquiry. Whoever will read or hear it with faith and love shall receive a great reward. May the Gooroo grant us the love of his feet and guard us in our last moments. The true Gooroo's praise be in the beginning and end. He has left his body according to his own will. O Sahib Singh the following verse was repeated by Narain Missur, who was a true servant of the Gooroo, viz., "Excellent is the Gooroo and excellent is the faith of seikhs!" We then went to Jummoo and the people of Doyra nation cut the heads of the two faithful seikhs. We seeing this felt a desire for retirement and betook ourselves to the houses of seikhs. I do not like Pundit or Brahman's house. I love the Gooroo, who has forgiven my ancestors. The Sahib Singh wrote those Sakhees in Sub 1781 and the last Sakhee was written in Sub 1821 and the following 4 verses were repeated by Narain Missur, viz., I wish that in every birth, the Gooroo may grant me his services as he had granted a "letter of order" to my ancestors, I wish to be born in that house, where I would be able to serve you. Even if I be born in a low or mean family, I may remain engaged in bringing straw for the devotees. O my Gooroo your religion is best, but it is in your hands to grant faith to the people. Protect my family, my wife, my children and all. It is proper to repeat the name of God and the word "Wah Gooroo;" do not feel disheartened, O devotees, for being born in high or low family. All the 100 Sakhees are finished.

THE END.